ADVANCED VALUE CLARIFICATION

HOWARD KIRSCHENBAUM, Ed.D.

UNIVERSITY ASSOCIATES
7596 Eads Avenue
La Jolla, Calif. 92037

TABLE OF CONTENTS

To Sid Simon and Merrill Harmin —
   who taught me about value clarification

To Jim Giordano —
   who taught me about objectives
   and how to achieve them

To Allan Glatthorn —
   who taught me about education
   as an experiment
   "Try it," he would say.
   "If it doesn't work,
   we can change it next year."

INTRODUCTION

Ten years ago, only a handful of individuals around the United States would have identified themselves as teachers or trainers of value clarification.* At that time, value clarification was an educational approach that was just becoming known—a few articles and research studies had been published, and a small number of workshops were being conducted each year around the country.

Today, the situation is entirely different. At least a dozen books, with total sales of over a million copies, and scores of articles have been published. Publishers are rushing to put something—occasionally anything—into print with the word *values* on the cover. Hundreds of college courses are being offered that either are specifically about value clarification or use value clarification as a major component or approach to an area of study. Tens of thousands of educators and others have participated in day-long or longer workshops in value clarification. Many individuals and groups regularly schedule, advertise, and conduct value-clarification workshops around the country, geared toward professional development or personal growth. It is hard to find a large professional conference that does not offer some speech or workshop relating to value clarification.

Yet, with this rapid increase in the use of value clarification, there has been little attention paid to the quality and types of training being utilized in this field. And the more value clarification spreads, the greater the problem of quality becomes. Because it is an approach that requires no esoteric knowledge and no particular professional degrees

---

*Over the past decade the terms "value clarification" and "values clarification" have been used with equal frequency. In this volume the author, who prefers the latter, has agreed to adopt the former so that the title will be consistent with another volume on this subject published by the same publisher.

1

to implement, because the proponents of value clarification have always encouraged its widespread use, and because it is a relatively simple approach to utilize initially, it seems as though it should be a relatively easy approach to teach to others. Thus, many people who have experienced a brief workshop in value clarification or who have had some initial success using it with their own students, clients, or children conclude, "Why, this is so simple, I could offer my own workshop on value clarification." And often it works out very well. The person does quite a good job of it, and the participants go away with a sound understanding of the theory of value clarification and the ability to utilize many of the strategies or activities.

But often it does not work out so well. What seemed to be a simple enough approach when experienced by a workshop participant turns out to pose many new problems to the would-be trainer. For behind the simple techniques of the method is an important set of attitudes and hypotheses about the nature of human growth and development, along with many skills in human relations, workshop design, and group dynamics. Without these attitudes or these skills, training in value clarification produces unexpected and undesirable consequences. Participants leave the workshop thinking of value clarification as simply a set of cute but superficial games or gimmicks. Or they see it as a new way of moralizing to children—teaching them the "right" values, the *teacher's* values. Or they see it as something to do separately from everything else: "It's Friday, time for value clarification."

Since 1968, I have been very much involved in the development and dissemination of value clarification, and therefore I have mixed feelings about the events just described—pleasure and pride over the many fine training efforts that are taking place, sadness and dismay over those training efforts, a minority, that result in "turned off" participants and misunderstandings of the approach. Had we anticipated how quickly value clarification would catch on, my colleagues and I might have taken additional steps in our dissemination efforts. Although advanced value-clarification workshops have dealt, in part, with the subject of training, this has never been explored in depth or with a large number of people. To date, I know of no publications on this subject.

Therefore, this volume is addressed directly to the many trainers of value clarification—workshop leaders, in-service teachers, consultants, college teachers, and others who train people to use the value-clarification approach or who offer workshops under that name. It is also addressed to classroom teachers and parents, who, in another sense, are value-clarification trainers—designing experiences to help students and children use the valuing process in their own lives. While several of the chapters are written specifically for trainers and workshop leaders, the bulk of this volume is also relevant to the classroom teacher or parent who has had previous experience with value clarification. It is my hope that this book will offer practical help on a complex task. It comes out of my own experience working with value clarification both in the classroom and in more than seventy two-day (or longer) value-clarification workshops and over a hundred shorter presentations and programs with groups of teachers, students, social workers, counselors, administrators, business people, police officers, ministers, parents, and others, in this country, Canada, and abroad, with groups of many races and religions. It is enhanced by valuable learnings from many colleagues, especially Sid Simon and Merrill Harmin, my original teachers in value clarification. It is the best of what I know about training in value clarification, but it is by no means the last word. I hope it will initiate a good deal more discussion, design, and research in an area that is vital to the future of value clarification and, I think, to education in general.

PART I:

THEORY AND RESEARCH

Chapter 1

CLARIFYING VALUE CLARIFICATION: SOME THEORETICAL ISSUES

Since the publication of *Values and Teaching* (Raths, Harmin, & Simon) in 1966, "value clarification" has become an extremely popular approach in education and in other helping professions. As with all new theories and techniques that enjoy widespread popularity, value clarification has generated its share of criticisms and misunderstandings. Among other things, value clarification has been called "hedonistic," "superficial," "relativistic," "value free," and "devoid of any cogent theoretical base." On the other hand, along with the criticism has come acclaim from thousands of teachers, parents, counselors, and others, who report that this same approach has been of significant help to them both in their work and in their personal lives. How can these conflicting views be reconciled? Is value clarification merely a helpful "tool" or educational technique, or does it really contain profound implications for human growth and development and for the entire educational process?

It is possible that those of us closest to value clarification have contributed to the misunderstandings and criticisms by not taking enough time to deal seriously with these issues. Thus, it is appropriate that this book concern itself with some of the more theoretical issues raised both by the critics and by the proponents of value clarification. After discussing the social context out of which value clarification has grown, I will present a somewhat different perspective on what value clarification is. Against this background, I can then respond directly to the theoretical issues referred to above.

CONFUSION AND CONFLICT

How do adults help young people (and one another) deal with such "value-rich" areas of confusion and conflict as politics; religion; fam-

7

ily; friends; work; leisure; love, sex; male/female roles; race, poverty, energy, etc.; health; money; personal habits; and so on?

One way might be to *moralize* to them: to gently or forcefully, subtly or harshly, tell them what to do, how to think, what is right or wrong, good or bad. Except that the teacher down the hall might be telling them something different. So might their parents, their ministers, their peer group, the media, movie stars, sports heroes, politicians, and advertisements. In fact, they are already being bombarded from all sides with different messages about what values to pursue, what goals to strive for in order to be successful, to belong, to be popular, to succeed with the other sex. We could add our input, certainly. But, then, how does the young person sort it all out?

Many do not. Often, young people grow into adulthood filled with contradictory values and inconsistent beliefs and behaviors. They become easy prey to the ad man's version of reality, the demagogue's lie, or the peer group's pressure toward complacency and mediocrity.

We could *model* a set of values, be a living example of what we believe. Most of us will try. One of the best ways to teach anything is to present a concrete example of it. And young people today are quick to spot adults who say one thing and do another. The problem with this approach is that there are too many models modeling too many different values—different goals, life styles, speech patterns, moral codes, orientations toward work and play, life and death. Which models are the real teachers, which the charlatans? How does the young person decide?

We could very well despair of being any help at all. We could take a laissez faire stance, throw up our hands, let them go their own way, and hope for the best. But it would be a naïve hope. Removing the moralizers or the models does not make growing up any simpler, does not turn confusion to clarity, does not teach anyone anything—except maybe that no one cares.

If we do care, we *will* model our values. But we can go a step further. We can teach young people (and one another) a *process* for clarifying and developing values—a process that they can use throughout their lives. We can teach a *set of valuing skills* that will serve young people long after they are beyond our immediate sphere of influence.

THE SEVEN PROCESSES

For several years, my colleagues and I have attempted to identify such a process, or set of valuing skills, and under the name of *value clarifica-*

tion, or *values clarification*, have encouraged educators, parents, and helping professionals to become actively involved in helping young people learn that process. Raths, Harmin, and Simon (1966) first explicated the process in their book *Values and Teaching*, in which they described seven subprocesses that lead toward value clarity. These subprocesses are (1) choosing from alternatives; (2) thoughtfully considering the consequences of alternatives; (3) choosing freely; (4) prizing and cherishing; (5) publicly affirming; (6) acting repeatedly; and (7) acting with a pattern or consistency. The seven subprocesses were also described as "criteria" for a "value." Subsequent publications explored new strategies to teach the seven subprocesses (Simon, Howe, & Kirschenbaum, 1972) and ways to combine value clarification with traditional school curricula (Harmin, Kirschenbaum, & Simon, 1973).

In a sense, the very term "value clarification" has contributed to some misunderstanding, implying to some people the goal of simply clarifying or "being clear" about one's values and implying to others a hedonistic lack of interest in anyone else's values; that is, to be clear about one's own values is enough. But this has never been the case. A concern for the *consequences* of one's position—both personal and social—has always been central to the clarifying process. From the beginning, value clarification has never encouraged a static "clarity"; instead, it is the *ongoing development* of one's values, including actions taken on them, that is valued.

Nevertheless, in recent years some misgivings have arisen about Raths' conception of the seven processes of valuing, or the criteria for a value. One problem is with the concept of criteria. Although useful theoretically, the concept is not operational. *How* proud must someone be of a belief before it may be considered a "value"? How *many* alternatives must be considered before the "alternatives" criterion is satisfied? How *often* must action be repeated? And so on. No one can say except the individual, and that individual's concern is to use the valuing processes wherever and whenever appropriate, not to achieve some theoretical goal of an "official value." More important, the seven subprocesses seem insufficient to fully comprehend the valuing process; that is, the means by which values are clarified and developed. A more recent formulation of the valuing process (Kirschenbaum, 1973) is based on Raths' original seven processes and is consistent with them, but it goes further in expanding the concept of "valuing."

EXPANDING THE PROCESS

The valuing process as defined here is *a process by which we increase the likelihood that our living in general or a decision in particular will, first, have positive value for us, and, second, be constructive in the social context.*[1] The use of the valuing process does not guarantee a good decision for ourselves or society; it merely increases the likelihood. The valuing process has five *dimensions*, each containing several subprocesses. The five dimensions are not discrete psychological processes; an individual can be engaged in all of them or some of them at the same time. It is helpful to separate them primarily as a means toward clarity of educational goals. The definitive list of valuing processes will probably never be written because anyone may legitimately choose to describe different parts of the elephant or to use different terminology. The dimensions described below include several processes to illustrate the dynamics of each valuing dimension.

Thinking

One way we can make better value decisions, according to our own or to society's standards, is to think. In this sense, anything we can do to help students learn to think and to reason more effectively is useful to them in their value development. Included in this dimension would be the skills of *thinking on various levels* (Bloom et al., 1956), *critical thinking* (Raths, 1967; Metcalf, 1974), *moral reasoning on the higher levels* (Kohlberg, 1968), *divergent or creative thinking* (Parnes, 1967), and others. Humanistic approaches to education, in their emphasis on the affective, often forget this dimension. It is an essential dimension of valuing if students are to learn to control their own lives, get along in a complex world, analyze advertising, propaganda, and information, and make crucial value decisions.

Feeling

Feelings can be an aid or an obstacle to effective thinking, decision making, and living. The traditional value-clarification process of knowing what we "prize and cherish" is an important part of value development, but only one part of the affective domain. People who feel good about themselves tend to be more effective by almost any set of criteria (Combs et al., 1971). People who are aware of their feelings are psychologically more mature and are able to achieve their goals more readily (Rogers, 1961). When we are not aware of or when we attempt to deny our feelings, we often find that they come out anyway—sometimes in surprising ways that can interfere with our conscious goals. People who have learned a process of discharging distressful feelings (emotional or physical hurt, anger, fear, embarrass-

---

[1]These two criteria are further defined in Chapter 2.

ment, etc.) have greater access to their full problem-solving capacity and are freer from the grip of patterned distress (Jackins, 1965). So again, anything we can do to help young people (and others) to strengthen their self-concepts and to deal with their feelings helps them learn a process that is part of their ongoing value development.

Choosing

Goal setting and *data gathering* are essential decision-making processes, after which *"choosing from alternatives"* and *"considering the consequences"* naturally follow. A longer menu does not insure that we will find something we like to eat; it just increases the odds. We cannot predict the future, but we can make an educated guess and lessen the chance of unexpected and undesirable consequences. *Choosing freely* is another valuing process, which involves distinguishing the pressures and consequences urging us toward certain choices drawn from our own subjective sense of which choice is best. Another choosing process that many teachers have been teaching their students is that of *achievement planning* (Alschuler et al., 1971), a process by which students learn strategies to increase the likelihood of achieving their goals. Luck need not determine whether we choose the "lady or the tiger"; it is possible to learn skills or processes that make us better choosers.

Communicating

Values do not develop in a vacuum, but through an ongoing process of social interaction. Therefore, the ability to *send clear messages* is an important valuing skill or process. To the extent that we can make our needs, values, or desires known to others, we increase the probability that others will respond in ways that meet those needs. In addition, appropriate sharing of our feelings and thoughts can have a clarifying effect (Jourard, 1964); that is, as we see how others respond to us and how we respond to public or private affirmation of our inner world, we learn more about the nature of the values we have chosen. Another valuing process here is empathy, active *listening*, or taking another's frame of reference. This process opens us up to new alternatives and decreases the likelihood that our values will rigidify and become self-defeating through denying or excluding the external world. *Conflict resolution* is a third valuing process under this dimension. Conflicts can end with several outcomes: none of the parties may actualize his or her values; one party may win and the other(s) lose; or all parties may achieve a satisfying solution, with all realizing most of the values they desired for that situation. Just being clear about our goals and values does not guarantee that we will achieve them—especially if we are living among other people. However, Thomas Gordon's work (1970, 1975) has been particularly helpful in teaching individuals communication skills and processes that can facilitate value and goal satisfaction for individuals and groups.

Acting

As value clarification has traditionally indicated, to *act repeatedly* upon our beliefs and to act *consistently* toward our goals increases the likelihood that our lives will have positive value to us. To this could be added the process of *acting skillfully* in the areas in which we do act. This would include academic, professional, and personal settings. To read, to change a tire, to cook a meal, to teach a class, to build a bridge, to clean up a polluted lake—whatever the field of our endeavor—*competence* helps increase the likelihood that the process and product will be not only personally satisfying but also socially productive.

Based on this expanded conception of the valuing process, value clarification can be defined as *an approach that utilizes questions and activities designed to teach the valuing process and that helps people skillfully to apply the valuing processes to value-rich areas in their lives*. With this definition in mind, it is possible to respond to some of the misconceptions often associated with value clarification.

VALUE CLARIFICATION—"VALUE FREE"? "RELATIVISTIC"?

In discussing value-rich areas, such as those mentioned at the beginning of this article, the teacher accepts all answers and does not try to impose his or her own views on the students. In that sense, the approach is "value free" and "relativistic." Responses are not judged as better or worse; each student's views are treated with equal respect.

But here the relativism stops. No matter what their viewpoint, *all* students are asked further clarifying questions. All are encouraged to continue using the valuing process. And it should be clear from the process that value clarification definitely promotes the values of thinking, feeling, choosing, communicating, and acting. Moreover, it values certain types of thinking, feeling, choosing, communicating, and acting. Thinking critically is regarded as better than thinking noncritically. Considering consequences is regarded as better than choosing glibly or thoughtlessly. Choosing freely is considered better than simply yielding to authority or peer pressure.

We can go even a step further (and I think we have erred in not making this explicit often enough); that is, toward what end are these valuing processes better than their counterparts? Here again, there are certain value judgments implicit in each process. If we urge critical thinking, then we value rationality. If we support moral reasoning, then we value justice. If we advocate divergent thinking, then we value creativity. If we uphold free choice, then we value autonomy or freedom. If we encourage "no-lose" conflict resolution, then we value equality. Some of these values are "instrumental" values and others are "terminal" values (Rokeach, 1971); for instance, the instrumental value of rationality is a means toward the terminal or end value of justice. In any case, all these "larger" values are clearly implicit in the valuing process. Thus, if called before the bench, we could only say that value clarification is not and never has been "value free."

THE QUESTION OF ABSOLUTES

On what authority, then, do we propose a system that has at its core the values of justice, equality, and freedom? This question and others generally come from two sources—the church and the cognitive-developmental psychologists.

To the church, we must say, "We don't know." Many advocates of value clarification do believe that there are absolute values, that is, absolute truths about the universe or values that everyone should hold for reasons that transcend rationality. They look to a higher authority to answer questions of ultimate values. Other advocates of value clarification do not believe this; they believe human beings must be the ultimate source for value decisions. Value clarification cannot solve this dilemma—it does not propose to answer all questions of human existence, including the origin and design of the universe. It does attempt to describe a valuing process and to say that if people use the process they will experience more positive value in their living and will be more constructive in the social context.

To the cognitive developmentalists dealing with moral reasoning, it could be said: "Simply because your research indicates that Kohlberg's sixth stage of moral reasoning is the product of a sequential, irreversible, cross-cultural sequence of human development, it is not proven that justice should be a universal value, maybe even the highest value. Physical disintegration and death are also sequential, more or less irreversible, and cross-cultural, but that does not mean we should encourage the process. What you have shown—and your work is important—is that if we provide certain conditions for people (e.g., moral reasoning at one level beyond their own), they will grow in certain predictable directions. Similarly, a physical educator could tell us that if we provide the right conditions for children, we could have almost everyone running a five-minute mile. And the behaviorists have demonstrated that if we provide the right conditions of reinforcement, we can get pigeons to play ping pong. This does not mean necessarily that, ipso facto, all pigeons should play ping pong, all people should run the five-minute mile, or all people should reason morally. The reason we think we should teach students how to reason morally is that we value justice. We can give lengthy reasons *why* we value justice, but we cannot *prove* that it is valuable. No amount of research can do that."

A THEORETICAL BASE FOR VALUE CLARIFICATION

Considering value clarification as the expanded process that has been described (but keeping in mind that this is merely an elaboration on what it always has been), it should be clear that value clarification is supported by a significant grounding in psychological theory and research. Research and theory in the areas of moral reasoning, critical thinking, creativity and problem solving, self-concept, psychotherapy, achievement motivation, group dynamics, helping relationships, and skill training, to name a few, has burgeoned in the last few decades. We still have an enormous amount to learn, and a separate book could be written on the research possibilities inherent in this presentation, but the fact remains that whatever research and theory exists to support any of these separate areas of study also supports value clarification.

Even in the traditional area of value clarification, as defined by the seven processes set forth by Raths, Harmin, and Simon (1966), there is an ever-increasing amount of research that can be cited (Kirschenbaum, 1975, describes eighteen recent studies). Given our increasing knowledge of the nature of human growth and development, future studies might focus on the important question of how value-clarification experiences can be more effectively sequenced, adapted, and combined with other approaches.

CONCLUSION

One may wonder whether value clarification, when thought of as a separate educational approach, continues to be a useful concept. Many different approaches, both cognitive and affective, have a part to contribute to the goal of fuller value development. It seems that in expanding our concept of the valuing process, we begin to develop a picture of a well-rounded person and soon find ourselves asking: What does it mean to be a mature or effective human being? What are humans potentially capable of becoming—physically, intellectually, and emotionally? In medicine and psychology, especially, we are discovering each year new areas of human potential, new abilities to extend life, to communicate verbally and nonverbally, to operate on different brainwave levels and perhaps in other psychic realms. One of the oldest philosophical questions—toward what end should humans strive?—is raised for us anew by these amazing discoveries of what actually is possible.

I would hope that value clarification and all the other approaches devoted to humanizing education will work together in an effort to better understand human growth and development and, based on this understanding, create better living and learning environments. Professional jealousy, competition, economic interests, or attitudes of "My approach is better than yours" should not be allowed to interfere with such important work.

REFERENCES

Alschuler, A. S., Tabor, D., & McIntyre, J. *Teaching achievement motivation*. Middletown, Conn.: Education Ventures, 1971.

Bloom, B. S. et al. *The taxonomy of educational objectives: Handbook I: The cognitive domain*. New York: David McKay, 1956.

Combs, A. W., Avila, D. L., & Purkey, W. W. *Helping relationships: Basic concepts for the helping professions*. Boston: Allyn & Bacon, 1971.

Gordon, T. *Parent effectiveness training*. New York: Peter Wyden, 1970.

Gordon, T. *Teacher effectiveness training*. New York: Peter Wyden, 1975.

Harmin, M., Kirschenbaum, H., & Simon, S. B. *Clarifying values through subject matter*. Minneapolis, Minn.: Winston Press, 1973.

Jackins, H. *The human side of human beings*. Seattle, Wash.: Rational Island Publishers, 1965.

Jourard, S. M. *The transparent self*. New York: D. Van Nostrand, 1964.

Kirschenbaum, H. *Beyond values clarification*. Upper Jay, N.Y.: National Humanistic Education Center, 1973.

Kirschenbaum, H. *Current research in values clarification*. Upper Jay, N.Y.: National Humanistic Education Center, 1975.

Kohlberg, L. The child as a moral philosopher. *Psychology Today*, September, 1968.

Metcalf, L. E. (Ed.). *Values education: Rationale, strategies & procedures, 41st yearbook*. Council of Social Studies, 1971.

Parnes, S. J. *Creative behavior guidebook*. New York: Charles Scribner's, 1967.

Raths, L. E., Harmin, M., & Simon, S. B. *Values and teaching*. Columbus, Ohio: Charles E. Merrill, 1966.

Raths, L., Wasserman, S., Jonas, A., & Rothstein, A. M. *Teaching for thinking*. Columbus, Ohio: Charles E. Merrill, 1967.

Rogers, C. R. *On becoming a person*. Boston: Houghton Mifflin, 1961.

Rokeach, M. Persuasion that persists. *Psychology Today*, September, 1971.

Simon, S. B., Howe, L., & Kirschenbaum, H. *Values clarification: A handbook of practical strategies for teachers and students*. New York: Hart, 1972.

Chapter 2

TEACHING VALUE-CLARIFICATION THEORY: SOME TECHNIQUES

Technically, value clarification is a *theory*, that is, a series of related and testable hypotheses. Louis Raths' original theory (Raths, Harmin, & Simon, 1966) suggested that apathetic, flighty, overconforming, overdissenting behavior, which accompanies confusion and conflict in values, can be changed to more zestful, purposeful, committed, consistent, critically thinking behavior as a result of value-clarifying experiences. Another hypothesis within the theory suggests that if a portion of time is taken from the facts and concepts level of teaching and is placed on the value level, the result will lead not only to value clarification but to an equal or greater amount of facts-and-concepts-level learning (Harmin, Kirschenbaum, & Simon, 1973). Additional hypotheses could be extracted from the literature.

The expanded concept of the valuing process outlined in the previous chapter adds yet another hypothesis to the overall theory of valuing. It suggests that the valuing process leads not only to a greater sense of personal value in one's decisions and general living (and, therefore, less apathy, flightiness, etc.) but also to more socially constructive behavior.

Without this type of theory as a foundation, value clarification cannot be much more than a series of unrelated games or gimmicks—a point that will be discussed further after looking at various ways to teach the theory.

Because it is more precise to think from the point of view of personal experience, much of the following material in the book is written in the first person. It is my intention, though, that readers will generalize from my experience to fit their own needs, and will apply my thoughts and suggestions in whatever way is most useful to them.

VALUE NEEDS

I frequently begin a workshop or presentation by describing or pointing out the need for work in the area of values. First I list the value-rich areas of confusion and conflict (politics, religion, family, friends, love and sex, etc.) on the chalkboard or on a piece of newsprint. I do this before the session begins, both to save time while I am speaking and to avoid establishing the typical teacher-student expectations associated with a slow-speaking teacher writing on the board. Depending on the situation, I will take from one to ten minutes to explain the list. I might simply call it to people's attention, saying, "Young people (or whoever the target group happens to be) have many areas of confusion and conflict in their lives—areas such as politics, religion, etc." and go right on to the next point. Or I might amplify on several or all of the areas by pointing to some of the questions or decisions facing individuals, more or less playing the role of a young person asking questions or wondering about religion, or work, or love and sex. If I happen to be working with a group with a particular focus—drugs, sexuality, work, college choice, etc.—I would still be inclined to call their attention to the entire list of areas, but to emphasize the area the group is most interested in and talk about the confusion and conflict facing people in that particular area. This also helps to make the point later that drug decisions or sexuality decisions, for example, are value decisions, and the same valuing process we use in one area of confusion and conflict can be used to deal with all the other areas as well.

"How do we help (young) people with areas of confusion and conflict in their lives?" With this question, I either end my theory presentation for the time being or make the transition to the next part of the theory. Occasionally, I give a ten-minute presentation like the preceding at the beginning of the workshop and say something like "We'll be exploring this question of how we help people with confusion and conflict in values throughout the workshop. It will be the theme of our time together. I'll say more about this later, but now let's do some activities that will begin to help us get to know one another (or learn some specific approaches)." Or I continue right then with more theory.

My timing and sequencing depend entirely on the situation. In a short presentation, I may briefly touch on almost every aspect of value-clarification theory, hoping that people will be impressed enough by the overview to want to return later for a more thorough exploration. On the other hand, I may be teaching a workshop or course or unit on value clarification that will last several days or weeks. In that case, I may choose to go more slowly, covering theoretical issues in greater depth, building strategies around each part of the theory. For example, I could have the participants list the areas of confusion and conflict and then code their lists: "1.—this area presents considerable confusion and conflict in my life; 2.—this area presents a little confusion and conflict in my life; 3.—this area is neither a source of confusion nor a source of much satisfaction in my life; 4.—this area is mostly a source of satisfaction in my life." The issues of timing and sequencing various segments of a workshop or presentation will be dealt with in greater detail in Part II, which discusses ways to design value-clarification training experiences.

WAYS OF WORKING WITH VALUES

Having posed the problem and asked how we can help, I like to point out that moralizing, laissez faire, and modeling are traditional approaches to dealing with values and that none of them accomplishes the all-important goal of teaching people a process they can use throughout their lives. I try to do this without making moralizers feel guilty or defensive. I am sincere when I say that there may be a great deal of wisdom and caring coming from a moralizer, but that moralizing does not effectively teach the valuing process.

It is often helpful to use a continuum to illustrate various ways of trying to help a person with his or her values. The theme of the continuum I use is "degree of directiveness."

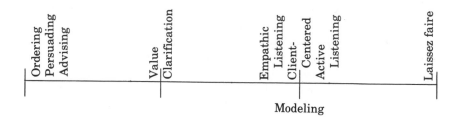

On one end of the continuum I write "laissez faire" and describe that non-approach. On the other end of the continuum I write "ordering" and immediately in front of that "persuading" and right next to that "advising." Although these various approaches to moralizing have differing degrees of directiveness, they all belong at the directive end of the continuum. Then one-third into the continuum from "laissez faire" I place "modeling" and explain that modeling is a type of involvement but not a *direct* involvement with the other person, and I point out the advantages of modeling, trying to leave the impression that this is a useful approach but not the only one. At the same point as "modeling" I write the phrases "emphathic listening," "client-centered," and "active listening," and describe these widely used counseling alternatives (Rogers, 1951; Gordon, 1970). Then one-third of the distance in from the directive end of the line I place "value clarification" and explain that value clarification is less directive than the moralizing alternatives because it does not presuppose any particular outcome for the person; rather, it allows the person to make his or her own decision. But value clarification is more directive than modeling or emphathic listening because it suggests that it would be helpful for a person to use certain valuing processes in reaching a decision.

THE VALUING PROCESS

Whether I list the various ways of trying to help with values or use the continuum approach just described, I save the discussion of value clarification until last. This allows me to make a transition to the next part of the theory—an explanation of what the valuing process does and what the other approaches do not teach. It also allows me to postpone an explanation of the valuing process until a later time, if I wish to.

There are many different ways to introduce the valuing process—whether one is describing Raths' seven criteria/processes or Kirschenbaum's five dimensions of the valuing process. One way is simply to deliver a straight lecture: I talk, they listen. I also post or write out a chart with the processes clearly listed. Sometimes I have a handout with the processes outlined in it. The point is, it really helps if a person can visualize what I am saying. Both concepts of valuing are rather elegant in their simplicity, and seeing them on paper or on a chart helps to dramatize this fact and fix it in the participants' memory.

The Values Grid strategy (#2)[1] is another graphic way of introducing the seven processes.

Sometimes I use what I call an "experiential lecture."[2] This means I present some of the information and then involve the participants in an experience that helps them personalize what they have heard. (It is actually teaching on the "third level.") For example, I may describe the process of "prizing and cherishing," then ask people to take turns, with

---

[1]A number in parentheses following the name of a strategy refers to the number of that strategy in Simon, Howe, and Kirschenbaum's (1972) *Values Clarification: A Handbook of Practical Strategies*.

[2]For a description of the experiential lecture technique, see J. W. Pfeiffer & J. E. Jones (Eds.), *The 1976 Annual Handbook for Group Facilitators*, La Jolla Calif.: University Associates, 1976, pp. 109-110.

their partners, talking about what they did that they prized or cherished during the last week. Or I might describe the five dimensions of valuing and ask them to rank the five dimensions in order, from those they feel they use most effectively to those with which they feel least effective or competent. When considering the valuing process as the primary subject matter, there is no end to the value questions that participants can be asked to help them relate that "subject matter" to their own lives.

I used to lecture on Raths' seven processes, arranging them under the three headings of Prizing, Choosing, and Acting. Since formulating the five dimensions of the valuing process (see Chapter 1), I have gone back and forth between two ways of presenting this newer version. Sometimes I list only the five dimensions—Thinking, Feeling, Choosing, Communicating, and Acting—and give examples of the various subprocesses as I discuss each major dimension. More recently, I have utilized a handout that lists the five dimensions, with the subprocesses under each dimension. By having the lecture outlined right in front of them, participants seem able to follow it much more easily. In addition, the outline is then available for later reference. However, Raths' seven processes have three major dimensions and seven processes of valuing. The expanded concept has five major dimensions and, as I usually explain it, eighteen processes of valuing. I may prefer the later concept, but I do not want to confuse or bore the participants. At this writing, however, I am reasonably pleased with the results of using the handout.

VALUE CLARIFICATION

Once the valuing process is explained, I can give a better picture of what I mean by value clarification. It is an approach that uses *questions or activities designed to help people learn the valuing process and apply it to value-rich areas in their own lives.* There are four primary ways in which value clarification can accomplish this goal. Barbara Glaser-Kirschenbaum uses the following simple diagram to graphically illustrate the four facets of the value-clarification approach.

Stated simply, the four applications may be described as follows. First, value clarification uses the "clarifying question," which is simply a question, asked at the appropriate time, that helps people learn to use a valuing process and to "clarify" some particular area in their lives. Second, there is the "clarifying interview," which uses a whole series of clarifying questions or activities to help people explore and clarify in depth some particular decision or choice they are facing.

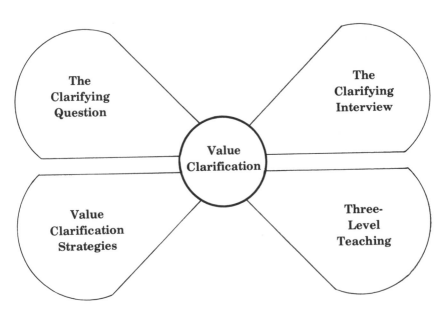

(This is not psychotherapy, but rather a process that focuses on the conscious elements involved in decision making, including one's readily accessible feelings.) In fact, value clarification originally began with an emphasis on the clarifying question and interview. Third, value clarification uses "strategies" or activities that are designed to help individuals or groups learn the valuing process and apply it to life areas of confusion and conflict. Finally, value clarification can be applied to subject matter—whether school subjects, such as English or science, religious studies, or such topical areas as drug use, sexuality, and so on. In this sense, value clarification provides models and examples of how to teach these subjects so that traditional content goals are served, while at the same time providing students the opportunity to learn the valuing process and use it to help relate the subject matter to their own value development.

In short workshops it is useful simply to enumerate sources that people can turn to in order to pursue these applications further. For example, an extensive treatment of the clarifying question and clarifying interview is presented in the book *Values and Teaching* (Raths, Harmin, & Simon, 1966); large selections of value-clarification strategies are offered in the books *Values Clarification: A Handbook of Practical Strategies* (Simon, Howe, & Kirschenbaum, 1972) and *A Practical Guide to Value Clarification* (Smith, 1977). For a thorough treatment of subject matter application, there is *Clarifying Values Through Subject Matter* (Harmin, Kirschenbaum, & Simon, 1973). In longer workshops, it is probably wise not to clutter up the theory presentation with these resources; instead, it might be a good idea to mention them at a later time.

Outcomes

What is accomplished by using value clarification? The theory suggests that if value clarification is used consistently, it leads to decisions and ways of living that are more likely to be personally satisfying and socially constructive.

"Personally satisfying" means that our living has value for us. We prize and cherish more of our choices, beliefs, and activities; we experience a stronger self-esteem; we experience greater meaning in our lives; we are less apathetic and flighty, more purposeful and committed. This does not mean that we are always "happy." It means that we are living vitally, experiencing the richness of ourselves, others, and the world around us, as we move toward self-selected, meaningful goals.

To be "socially constructive," as used here, means to act in ways that promote the values of "life," "liberty" (that is, freedom, justice, and equality), and the "pursuit of happiness." While philosophers may continue to argue for centuries as to the precise meanings of words like *freedom, justice,* and *equality,* value-clarification theory will settle for a working definition of these terms as is explicitly stated in the Bill of Rights and the United Nations Declaration on the Rights of Man. Stated somewhat differently, to be socially constructive is to increase the likelihood that others may have lives that have value to *them,* so long as they do not infringe on the rights of others.

THE IMPORTANCE OF VALUE-CLARIFICATION THEORY

With this foundation, I feel comfortable launching into any of the four directions just mentioned. Participants have an understanding of why we are doing what we are doing at the workshop and what purposes these activities might serve back home. Of course, I come back to these points in many different ways throughout the workshop. I add new pieces of learning theory, developmental psychology theory, group dynamics theory, value-clarification research, and whatever else might be relevant at different points during the workshop or training session. But this foundation provides the basic structure on which everything else can understandably fit.

Without such a structure or set of goals in mind, what possible purpose would value clarification serve? One often hears such comments as "My students enjoy it," "Value-clarification strategies make our car rides pass more quickly," or "It keeps the kids interested during the last ten minutes of the school day." These may be useful side benefits of value clarification, but they are not its purpose. If a teacher or a trainer sees value clarification as no more than a set of games that help pass the time and keep the troops happy, the troops will develop a similar attitude about value clarification. They will see it as a filler, as fun and games, and will appreciate it to a point, but beyond that point they will start to wonder "What are we doing these silly (or stupid) games for? How is this going to help me get into college? Why should I answer all these questions you are asking me?"

On the other hand, when a teacher thoroughly understands and believes in the theory, he or she almost inevitably begins to teach the theory to the students. This of course is the goal. The theory behind value clarification is not a hidden theory. There are no secret purposes of value clarification that, if known, would render the strategies ineffective. On the contrary, value clarification works best when the goals are explicit or shared. I can be exploring a dilemma with my wife Barb, and she can ask me if I'd like some clarifying questions. Because we both know the goals and the ground rules, we can proceed efficiently without any sense of gimmickry or artificiality. Similarly in a classroom or group. When the participants have a shared sense of the nature of their value needs—including all the accompanying confusion, apathy, flightiness, etc.—when they have an understanding of the pros and cons of different approaches for helping people with value conflict, and when they understand the valuing process and the different ways it may be applied through value clarification, then value clarification is working at its best. It all begins with the trainer, who understands value-clarification theory and who makes the communication of that theory a top priority in his or her presentations and workshops.

REFERENCES

Gordon, T. *Parent effectiveness training*. New York: Peter Wyden, 1970.

Harmin, M., Kirschenbaum, H., & Simon, S. B. *Clarifying values through subject matter*. Minneapolis, Minn.: Winston Press, 1973.

Raths, L. E., Harmin, M., & Simon, S. B. *Values and teaching*. Columbus, Ohio: Charles E. Merrill, 1966.

Rogers, C. R. *Client-centered therapy*. Boston: Houghton Mifflin, 1951.

Simon, S. B., Howe, L., & Kirschenbaum, H. *Values clarification: A handbook of practical strategies*. New York: Hart, 1972.

Smith, M. *A practical guide to value clarification*. La Jolla, Calif.: University Associates, 1977.

Chapter 3

CURRENT RESEARCH IN VALUE CLARIFICATION

One often-heard criticism of value clarification is that it has no sound basis in research—that very little is known about whether the approach indeed accomplishes its stated objectives of helping people to clarify and develop their own values and value systems as well as helping them learn a valuing process that can serve them throughout their lives.

Early research on value clarification, as reported in a chapter in *Values and Teaching* (Raths, Harmin, & Simon, 1966), provided tentative support for the hypothesis that value-clarification experiences contributed to these goals. Most of the twelve studies reported used Raths' theoretical framework, which said that apathetic, flighty, inconsistent, overconforming, overdissenting, posing, and other "non-value-based" behavior would change in the direction of becoming more purposeful, consistent, and rational as a result of value-clarifying experiences. Although the results were not totally consistent, the direction of the findings tended to support Raths' theory. They also indicated that value clarification contributed to higher school achievement, presumably as a result of the students' greater clarity about goals and purposes.

These early findings, however, were far from conclusive. The size of the studies was usually quite small and controls were rarely adequate. Other flaws in methodology made it impossible to attribute changes to value clarification alone or called into question the reliability of the measurements. The authors were quite fair in describing

---

This chapter is a revised and expanded version of the author's *Recent research in values clarification*. Upper Jay, N.Y.: National Humanistic Education Center, 1974. Two descriptions have been revised and thirteen new studies added.

their results as lending some support to the value theory, but they also made it clear that much further research was needed and even indicated many of the specific questions that needed exploration. For a period of several years following the publication of *Values and Teaching*, events did not fulfill the authors' hopes that further research would follow. The efforts of those most involved in developing and promulgating the approach went toward further development of new value-clarification activities and of new applications to school and other settings. Only since colleges of education have begun to utilize value clarification in teacher education courses and graduate students have decided to conduct their doctoral research in this area, have we seen a resurgence of research on value clarification. Another source of new research efforts has its roots in drug-abuse education projects, which often use the value clarification methodology and usually are required to demonstrate some empirical results to their funding source.

The differences between the older and newer studies are much more apparent than are the similarities. The methodology is usually more sophisticated than that used in the majority of the earlier studies; the populations are often larger; there is a greater emphasis on value-clarification strategies used with classes and groups as opposed to clarifying questions with individuals (as was often the case previously); and the dependent variables being measured range further from Raths' "non-value-based" behaviors than before, including such items as self-esteem, self-actualization, drug use, and various classroom behaviors. It would be a mistake to exaggerate these differences, however. The newer studies are clearly in the tradition of the earlier research and can be seen as an extension of it, based on the changes value clarification has undergone in the past decade and on the changing concerns of the educational community.

Following are summaries of nineteen studies that have been completed in the last few years, many of them published or soon to be published. Many more such studies will undoubtedly emerge soon.* The studies are grouped under three headings: (1) outcomes of value clarification with students and other target populations; (2) outcomes of teacher training in value clarification; and (3) methodological developments.**

---

*The author would appreciate receiving copies of other studies on value clarification not included in the present review.

**Two additional studies not summarized here are Bloom (1970) and Quinn (1973).

OUTCOMES OF VALUE CLARIFICATION WITH STUDENTS AND OTHER TARGET POPULATIONS

Barman

Charles Barman (1974) and two colleagues each taught one experimental and one control class of high school biology students. The experimental groups were taught value-clarification lessons once a week for eighteen weeks; except for that, both groups received the same BSCS Yellow Version biology course. The value-clarification groups developed significantly (compared with the control groups) on cognitive achievement, measured both by the objective BSCS final exam and by student self-evaluation on behavioral objectives for the course. There was no significant difference between experimental and control groups on attitudes toward biology, science, and the affective domain.

Blokker, Glaser, and Kirschenbaum

In this project, coordinated by William Blokker (et al., 1976) under a grant from New York State's Education Department, experienced consultants were used to plan and implement each phase of the research and the teacher-training program. Marianne Simon carried out the training, and Jerome Platt and Marshall Swift supervised the evaluation. Twenty-two fourth- through sixth-grade teachers (in many buildings) spent five weeks utilizing the value-clarification approach for at least one hour a day with their classes in a unit called "All About Me," modified by each teacher for his or her own classroom. About 250 boys and 250 girls participated. Significant changes, lasting four weeks after the unit ended, were demonstrated in the students' improved decision-making ability as measured by Ojemann's Social Causality Test (1961), in their increased belief in their personal control over their own lives as measured by the Nowicki and Strickland Internal-External Control Scale (1973), and in their increased overt self-reliant behavior as measured by the revised Devereux Elementary School Behavior Rating Scale (Swift & Spivack, 1974). All these measures have been shown to correlate with low drug abuse. There were no significant changes in self-esteem as measured by the Cutick Self-Evaluation Form (1962). It was suggested that actual effective performance in the real world is necessary for improved self-esteem, and that the changes in decision-making ability and sense of personal control, etc., would lead to more effective behavior that only later would be translated to increased self-esteem. Unforeseen problems in the assignment of teachers to control groups rendered the control group data unusable; it is therefore impossible at this time to be sure the changes can be attributed to the value-clarification training.

Clarke et al.

The largest and most important study on value clarification to date (Clarke et al., 1974) took place in Visalia, California, under the sponsorship of Operation Future, a youth development and delinquency prevention organization with Jay Clarke as director. The population included 851 fifth through tenth graders, two groups of pregnant minors, two church groups, and sixty-five young people on probation. They were surveyed and rated as to their use of various nonprescribed drugs, their perception of themselves in reference to eight character traits associated with lack of value clarity (e.g., apathy, flightiness, etc.), and their school behavior. One significant finding was a high correlation between drug use and several of the low-valuing traits.

In the second part of their study, Clarke et al. measured the effect of value-clarification experiences on the character traits and on the students' use of drugs. The effect of the independent variable on the traits was mixed, with some of the experimental groups remaining the same, a few regressing slightly, and several making enormous gains, i.e., becoming less apathetic, etc. In the area of drug use, the gains were unmistakably significant, as indicated in a preliminary report that stated, "For the most part all groups reduced their intake of all drugs with the exception (in some groups) of alcohol." Not only were these results statistically significant, but in many cases the changes were dramatic in degree. Another dramatic set of findings showed how, without the use of value clarification in the control groups, there was a significant decline in the students' social adjustment. This brief summary barely scratches the surface of a complex study, the implications of which could be profound both for further research and for educational practice.

Covault

Thomas Covault (1973) measured the effect of value-clarification strategies on fifth-grade students' self-concepts and "related classroom coping and interacting behaviors." His population consisted of two experimental classes and two controls. He found that students who experienced eleven one-hour sessions of value clarification as compared with the controls (who received the same amount of time in physical education with the investigator): (1) improved in "self-concept" as measured by the Sears Self-Concept Scale, (2) improved in "initiation and self-direction of classroom activities," (3) improved in "positive attitude toward learning," and (4) decreased in the amount of apathetic, flighty, uncertain, inconsistent, drifting, overconforming, overdissenting, and role-playing behavior.

Gorsuch, Arno, and Bachelder

An experienced evaluation team conducted a carefully controlled study (Gorsuch, Arno, & Bachelder, 1976) on the effects of an extensive value-clarification program sponsored by the Akron, Ohio, and the National YMCA. They found that the values program (with fourth, fifth, and sixth-grade boys) led to significant changes in the groups which had the longer exposures to the program—the club groups which met throughout the year versus the brief summer camp experiences, the boys who experienced two years of the program versus one year. This suggests that those short studies—e.g., ten sessions—which show no changes may not be fair tests of the approach.

Although the data is varied, the major changes were in three areas. The boys in the value clarification program, compared to the controls, (1) shifted toward value which children generally see as desirable in their social environment and on which adults generally score higher than children of this age (while one may question the conformity contained within this criterion, Kohlberg suggests that social conformity is a transitional phase necessary to progress to a more internally-controlled ethical system), (2) increased the degree to which they saw as being deviant behavior that is normally defined as deviant within our culture, e.g., excessive use of alcohol (the norm is for children to become increasingly tolerant of deviant acts as they grow older), and (3) became more supportive of internalized values as contrasted with basing value decisions solely on external circumstances (clearly a major goal of value clarification).

Gray

Russell Gray (1975) taught a one-hour value-clarification session once a week for eleven weeks in four sixth-grade Catholic school classrooms. He spent an equal amount of time in three control classrooms, teaching two groups creative writing and tutoring the other (in small groups) in mathematics. He found no significant differences between the experimental groups and control groups on the Piers-Harris Children's Self-Concept Scale or on six of the seven items on a standard sociometric questionnaire. On the seventh item ("number of rejectees"), the control groups did better than the experimentals.

Guziak

John Guziak (1974) replicated the Covault study, cited above, and obtained essentially the same positive findings. Some small but interesting differences in the study were the following: (1) Guziak used only eight sessions, compared to Covault's eleven; (2) Guziak's control groups experienced a "well-organized music class," compared to Covault's physical education class controls; and (3) whereas Covault taught both experimental groups, Guziak taught one and had another school psychologist teach the other.

Kaufman

Marilyn Kaufman (1974), using a population of undergraduate junior and senior women, compared the effectiveness of (1) group career counseling (a credit class) that employed a combination of value clarification, decision making, and career-exploration activities, (2) one-to-one career counseling, and (3) no class or counseling. Both experimental groups did significantly better than the controls, and the value-clarification group method produced significantly better results than the one-to-one counseling on self-knowledge, knowledge of self in relation to career, and planning activities in seeking career information. Because the group experienced fourteen class hours plus out-of-class work, compared to an average of 1.3 sessions in one-to-one counseling, the significance of the findings lies not in the direct comparison of the two methods, but in a recognition of the differential benefits that motivated students achieve when they enter a value-oriented career-exploration class compared to when they enter individual counseling. This could have important implications for the priorities of career-counseling and placement programs.

Kelley

Felonese Kelley (1976) found that students of the six upper elementary school teachers who, following a training program, implemented value clarification in their classrooms, when compared with six elementary teachers who had no special training, improved significantly on measures of self-concept and sentiment toward school and showed no difference from the control group on a test of reading achievement. Since the control group teachers apparently received no special attention, it is impossible to say that the value clarification, per se, was responsible for the gains, as opposed to the special attention the teachers received.

Little

A small, unpublished study by R. J. Little (1975) showed how a value-clarification approach to driver education was more successful than a lecture approach in terms of student attitudes toward the course, attendance, and grades. The value-clarification class was taught by the experimenter; the other course was taught by a colleague committed to the lecture approach. The same text and testing procedures were used. The difference in attitude was statistically significant; the differences in attendance (99.13 percent vs. 96 percent) and grades (91.96 percent vs. 87.75 percent) were not calculated for significance.

Osman

Jack Osman (1974) used fifteen value-clarification strategies with eighty-eight future teachers in his college-level health-education classes. He found a significant difference between their scores on a pre- and post-test of Shostrom's Personal Orientation Inventory (a test of self-actualization). As he states, however, lack of a control group prevented coming to the conclusion that this finding was attributable to the experimental procedure (the value clarification). On other measures, using self-reports of the students, Osman found that "almost 50 percent of the students rated themselves as having become more involved in the valuing process since the course began. More than 80 percent expressed a greater awareness of their values. Almost half . . . stated that their speech had become more consistent with their actions as a result of their experiences in the course." The findings were all consistent with the values theory, but, again, the lack of controls calls into question the meaning of the findings. Perhaps the major contribution of the study was the investigator's early (1970) use of a reasonably well-known, reliable, paper-and-pencil measurement tool to assess the results of value clarification on a variable somewhat related to the values theory, i.e., self-actualization, as opposed to the more traditional measurements of the *content* of people's values.

Pracejus

Eleanor Pracejus (1975) compared gains in reading comprehension between one group of eighth graders who had twelve sessions of discussing stories using a value-clarification approach and one group reading the same stories and following the publisher's suggested discussion approach. The value-clarification group had significantly greater reading comprehension.

Rutkowski

David Rutkowski (1975) found that value-clarification strategies and "value level" treatment of subject matter tended to increase his high school chemistry students' positive attitudes toward science. Using the students as their own controls, he administered the instrument four times before beginning the experimental treatment and four times during it. The increase reached statistical significance during the value-clarification period, but lost its statistical significance on the last attitude test administered. A follow-up test would have helped determine how significant the attitude change really was.

Sklare

Gerald Sklare (1974) measured the effect of ten value-clarification classes on high school psychology students. One experimental class had the ten sessions on consecutive days, the other once a week over ten weeks. Two control classes received equal time of the normal psychology curriculum. There were no significant differences found between the experimental and control groups on the Rokeach Value Survey (measuring student value priorities) or on the Prince Differential Values Inventory (measuring value orientation from "traditional" to "emergent")—the value-clarification theory does not predict a change on these measures—or on a Dogmatism Scale. There was a significant difference in the "spaced" experimental group's gain in "value clarity" as measured by a variation on the Differential Values Inventory. In fact, it was a general trend in the study that the experimental group with the value clarification spaced over ten weeks showed greater changes than the experimental group with the ten consecutive sessions; however, this difference was not always statistically significant.

Wenker-Konner, Hammond, and Egner

Ronnie Wenker-Konner, Eileen Hammond, and Ann Egner (1973), in connection with the University of Vermont, Goddard College, and the South Burlington, Vermont, School District, employed a strict behavioral design to study the effect of value-clarification strategies on the participation rate of fifth graders. First, Raths' "non-value-based" behaviors, such as apathy, flightiness, etc., were translated into fifty-five discrete classroom behaviors. These, in turn, were grouped under five major headings: (1) active participation, (2) alternative behavior, (3) inappropriate verbal behavior, (4) refusal to participate, and (5) none of the above. A test of interrater reliability indicated an average of 99.7 percent agreement between the experimenter and an independent observer when both observers rated the same children at ten-second intervals. Ten children, unknown to the teacher, were selected for their lack of participation and their disruptive behavior and were observed for ten days to obtain a base-line score for their behavior. Then, for fifteen days, the teacher introduced value-clarification strategies for part of the day, for two days she ceased using it, and finally, for two days, she recontinued its use. The ten students were observed throughout the entire period. Careful analysis of the results indicated that during value-clarification activities, the students' active participation increased and their alternative behavior, inappropriate verbal behavior, and refusal to participate decreased (the change in all four categories was extreme), and, as predicted, there was no significant change in the random "none of these" category.

Wilgoren

Wilgoren (1973) contrasted the Raths-oriented value-clarification approach with the Oliver value-clarification approach, which uses more of a cognitive-confrontational model. Fifty undergraduate pre-service teachers who signed up for the experience were divided randomly into four groups—two experimental and two controls. The experimental period comprised seventy-five-minute sessions twice a week for six weeks. Both experimental groups showed a positive change in self-concept compared to the control groups, as shown by the Berger Self-Acceptance Scale (pre-test) and the Phillips Self Questionnaire (post-test). There was no difference apparent between the two approaches.

OUTCOMES OF TEACHER TRAINING IN VALUE CLARIFICATION

Betof

Edward Betof (1976), in the tradition of the Pozdol study reported below, surveyed 226 teachers (80 percent responded) who had been through 36 hours of value clarification training. He explored many questions Pozdol did not, finding, for example, that teachers thought they had implemented value clarification most successfully in the following ways (ranked in order): aiding students' personal growth, clarifying teaching philosophy and expanding teaching skills, facilitating teacher-student interaction, facilitating teacher-staff interaction, using value clarification within the curriculum, and aiding students' academic growth. The first four areas had the highest levels of implementation, the last two had moderate level, with about 50-60 percent of the sample indicating significant gains in these categories. Betof also found there were no demographic generalizations to be made about implementing value clarification, that is, teachers felt they were able to implement the approach regardless of their sex, class size, subject matter and grade levels, years of teaching experience, age, and level of graduate training completed. Many other individual questions of interest were explored.

Blokker, Glaser, and Kirschenbaum

This study, reported above, had one component that measured teacher response to the training and the teachers' implementation of the value-clarification unit. The majority were favorable in their response to value clarification and felt, in retrospect, that the four-day training program had prepared them adequately (44 percent-very much so, 52 percent-yes, 4 percent-somewhat) for teaching the value-clarification unit in the classroom. Sixteen percent felt they were very successful in implementing the unit; 36 percent, successful; and 44 percent, moderately successful. An important relationship yet to be explored would compare the outcomes of those teachers who felt they were more successful with the outcomes of those teachers who felt they were less successful. If it is demonstrated that the "more successful" group obtained better results, the claim that value clarification, when implemented successfully, produces positive results would be strengthened.

Curwin

Following a training program in value clarification for twenty-eight student-teachers of English or pre-service English teachers, Curwin (1972) conducted a careful analysis of their self-reports. These reports indicated that (1) the participants felt greater clarity on several aspects of teaching and English teaching; (2) they had somewhat greater awareness of the alternatives open to them as English teachers; (3) most of them would use most of the value-clarification activities with their students; and (4) the course was very useful to them. This study offered a real improvement from the "Did you like it or not?" type of feedback often gathered, and it pointed the way to a more careful type of field research and self-assessment that can help the educator decide to continue, discontinue, or modify a learning program. (The Pozdol study, reported later, took this approach one step further.)

Kirschenbaum

In this small study, the author (1970) measured the outcomes of a two-and-one-half-hour in-service meeting he conducted with eighty elementary and junior high school teachers in a New Jersey school district. They had had no previous formal exposure to value clarification, and since this was in 1970, there was scant literature they could have read. Using a group of students from the district, Kirschenbaum demonstrated the Voting (#3), Ranking (#4), Continuum (#8), Proud Whip (#11), and Public Interview (#12) strategies and then gave the teachers a chance to practice creating and experiencing the first four of the strategies in small groups. One month later, the teachers filled out an anonymous questionnaire, indicating which of the strategies they had used in their classrooms during that month and whether they planned to continue using them. Seventy-five percent indicated they had used one strategy, 50 percent had used two, 30 percent had used three, 12 percent had used four, and 8 percent had used all five. Eighty-two percent of the teachers who had used a particular strategy indicated they planned to continue using it.

Pozdol

Marvin Pozdol (1974) of Cleveland State University completed the most extensive evaluation to date of the results of teacher training in value clarification. He sent 200 former graduate students who had taken his introductory course on value clarification an anonymous questionnaire containing seventy-eight questions that covered their reactions to the course, its effects on their teaching and personal lives, their willingness to share resources with others, their future professional development plans, and so on. Most of the former students were elementary school teachers, with some middle school and a few high school teachers. The data are so rich and varied it would be impossible to summarize them. A few sample items are: "The requirement of tape recording some of my value-clarification sessions was worthwhile." Strongly Agree-35 percent, Agree-46 percent, Disagree-11 percent, Strongly Disagree-1 percent. "I use at least one value-clarification strategy each day." SA-4 percent, A-33 percent, D-53 percent, SD-5 percent. "I use at least one value-clarification strategy each week." SA-30 percent, A-50 percent, D-13 percent, SD-1 percent. "Since completing the value-clarification course I have searched for and read books, articles, and so on related to value-clarification." SA-21 percent, A-53 percent, D-20 percent, SD-1 percent. Of the 150 students who returned the questionnaire, the following numbers indicated they had used that semester some of the strategies that Pozdol had taught: Here and Now Wheel-49, Rank Order-120 (#4), Values Continuum-87 (#8), Public Interviews-51 (#12), I Wonder Statements-92 (#16), and so on. The overall results clearly indicated that the course had been successful, that teachers were using value clarification, that they felt it had helped them personally and professionally, and that they wished to pursue their learnings in this and related areas.

Redman

George Redman (1975) conducted an exploratory study with volunteers for value clarification training, in which he found that after 24 hours of training, when the teachers responded to a nine-minute conflict film, they showed significantly greater "openness," defined as (1) an identification with and/or support of the needs and interests of students as individuals and (2) a recognition that their assessments of the film were subjectively held. The selection of the sample and the lack of a control group make it difficult to generalize from these findings.

Smith

Bryan Smith (1973), in a study sponsored by the Florida State Department of Education, under a drug-education training project, measured the effectiveness of a group-centered value-clarification approach compared to a teacher-centered approach for teaching drug education to pre-service elementary teachers. The group-centered value-clarification group "was found to be superior in all ways measured." Namely, members of this group did more independent reading, scored higher on various affective and cognitive tests, and developed a greater sense of community, which enabled them to solve problems together more effectively. An unforeseen problem in the assignment of teachers to groups, however, raised the possibility that teachers assigned to the teacher-centered group and control group might have resented such placement, thereby biasing the results.

METHODOLOGICAL DEVELOPMENTS

In addition to shedding light on various outcomes of value-clarification experiences or teacher training, many of the studies reported above represent contributions to the methodology of value-clarification research. This section highlights studies that were primarily aimed at contributing some new measurement tool or approach for the study of a particular variable related to value clarification.

Raduns

Linda Raduns (1973) developed an instrument to measure the "here and now" status of value clarification in the area of ecology through the use of Raths' seven criteria. After administering the instrument to ninety-four college students taking an elective health education course emphasizing value-clarification strategies, the following hypotheses were confirmed: (1) the subjects did not hold clarified values in the area of ecology and (2) there is a difference in the value depending on whether it concerns what "others" should do or the action the person himself is willing to take in behalf of the value. The thesis points to an area of future valuable research—using Raths' seven criteria to measure the *extent of valuing* a person is engaging in, in general or with respect to a specific value-rich area.

Warger

Cynthia Warger (1976) developed a questionnaire to assess teachers' willingness to use value clarification and their ability to do so (while the questionnaire appears conceptually valid, its predictive validity was not tested). Forty-one questionnaires out of 115 were returned from two high school faculties (biased sample?). She found that while 53.7 percent of the respondents were *willing* to use value clarification and 34.2 percent had the *ability* to do so, only 17.1 percent had both the willingness and the ability to use the method. At the same time, 87.9 percent of the teachers indicated a willingness to participate in a value-clarification workshop. More than in its specific findings, this study represents a methodological contribution in its attempt to develop an attitude test that can predict the effective use of the value-clarification approach. It opens up for future study the whole question of "What attitudes are necessary for effectiveness in using value clarification?"

THE OVERALL SIGNIFICANCE OF THE RESEARCH

While most of the studies reported above can be criticized from several research perspectives, and I have occasionally done so in my descriptions of them, I find their combined weight to be very impressive. They lend considerable face validity to the hypothesis that: *if reasonably receptive teachers go through a competently led experience in value-clarification training, their energy and enthusiasm for teaching will be increased, and a large percentage will return to their classrooms and implement the approach so that their students will be positively influenced on various dimensions of personal and/or academic growth.*

Critics of the research might challenge each and every phrase in this hypothesis. For example, "reasonably receptive" will evoke the criticism that reasonably receptive people are likely to benefit from most any new method or innovation. What about the large number of teachers who are not receptive to value clarification?

Actually, compared to many innovations, teachers are unusually receptive to value clarification. I have often worked with conservative faculty groups and been very impressed to see how, within a few short hours, the large majority of teachers became very involved with the valuing strategies. Akron, Ohio would be considered by most, I think, fairly typical of middle America. Chapter 8 describes how my colleagues and I worked with this school system and how over the years more and more teachers became receptive to participating in value-clarification workshops. The idea that there is one new method which can be imposed on all people—the receptive and resistent alike—and that this method will achieve universally positive results in sheer fantasy. That may work when putting fluoride in a town's water supply, but innovations in human systems simply do not work that way. People have got to be receptive to change to make the change work, and value clarification seems well suited in this respect because (1) so many people are receptive to it to begin with and (2) experiencing the strategies tends to lessen resistence and/or increase receptivity among those who initially are not receptive to the idea.

"A competently led experience" is another important part of the hypothesis, but I see little to argue about it. It would be expecting a lot of an approach to require that incompetent training produce effective new behaviors in teachers.

Another criticism will be: "Perhaps it was the teachers' enthusiasm, not the value clarification itself, which was responsible for the changes." My response is that anyone who has ever conducted in-service training for school faculties knows how difficult it is to get a group of teachers enthusiastic about a new approach and to carry that enthusiasm over into behavioral change in the classroom. If the enthusiasm that a value-clarification workshop generates is a factor in its success, I do not apologize for it, I welcome it.

Others will point out that the research is equivocal. Some studies show greater changes in the experimental groups, others show no difference in the experimental and control groups. Some show changes in the affective area, but not the cognitive, some show the reverse, some show both, and some show neither. This is to be expected. For value clarification (or most other approaches) to be unequivocally effective, it must be used effectively over time, probably over many years (this is a researchable question itself). In many of these studies, the experimental treatment lasted only about ten or twelve hours. In many of the studies the teachers were using value clarification for the very first time, while the control-group teachers were using the approaches they had used for years. It is remarkable that so many studies did show positive changes, under the circumstances. It is also significant that in no studies did the experimental groups regress or do more poorly than the controls. Whereas the results in any one or a few studies might be termed "equivocal," the directionality of the overall findings can only be considered highly consistent. The most serious and frequent criticism will score the lack of adequate control groups in many (not all) of the studies. Since the teachers and students who experienced value clarification thereby became a "special" group, unless there are control groups who get some sort of special treatment, then one cannot tell if it was the value clarification or the sense of "specialness" which produced the results. Similarly, unless adequately controlled for, the selection of teachers for the value-clarification groups may also create a biased sample of teachers, not typical of the majority.

One response to this is to acknowledge its accuracy and to encourage more carefully controlled studies in the future. I share this view. But there is another response which poses a serious challenge, in return, to those who feel that human knowledge can proceed only through carefully controlled experiments. An alternative scenario for progress in this area suggests that if a new approach seems to have worked well for, let us say, a dozen teachers, then let us not worry about control groups but instead give another twelve teachers a chance to learn and utilize the new approach. If our evaluation indicates that twenty-four teachers now seem to be using the approach successfully, let us increase the number to one hundred. And if it works with one hundred teachers, why not try it with five hundred or a thousand, carefully checking our results as we go, to see that we are achieving our goals and that no undesirable side effects are resulting? If a thousand, why not ten thousand?

I am not suggesting that controlled research stop (it can be done simultaneously), but only that it not be allowed to halt progress which can proceed very well by alternate routes.

I shall not attempt to deal with all the possible criticisms of the value-clarification research. As I have indicated, much of it is valid and there is a need for more and better research in this area. On the other hand, it would be a mistake to become apologetic regarding the gains value clarification has demonstrated in the research such as it is. The accumulation is impressive enough to bolster our confidence in the approach and allow us to proceed, as still new studies are undertaken and new knowledge is generated.

REFERENCES

Barman, C. R. *The influence of values clarification techniques on achievement, attitudes and affective behavior in high school biology.* Unpublished doctoral dissertation, University of Northern Colorado, 1974.

Betof, E. H. *The degree of implementation of values clarification by classroom teachers following an intensive thirty-six hour workshop.* Unpublished doctoral dissertation, Temple University, 1976.

Blokker, W., Glaser, B., & Kirschenbaum, H. Values clarification in health education. *Health Education* April-May 1976.

Bloom, R. L. Development of competency in the use of value-clarification techniques by master of arts in teaching interns for the clarification of value-related problem behavior of selected secondary school students. *Dissertation Abstracts International*, 1970, *30*, 2875A.

Clarke, J. et al. *Operation future: Third annual report.* San Diego, Calif.: Pennant Educational Materials, 1974.

Covault, T. *The application of value clarification teaching stategies with fifth grade students to investigate their influence on students' self-concept and related classroom coping and interacting behaviors.* Unpublished doctoral dissertation, Ohio State University, 1973.

Curwin, R. *The effects of training in values clarification upon twenty-eight student-teachers and pre-service teachers of English.* Unpublished doctoral dissertation, University of Massachusetts, 1972.

Cutick, R. A. *Self-evaluation of capacities as a function of self-esteem and the characteristics of a model.* Unpublished doctoral dissertation, University of Pennsylvania, 1962.

Gorsuch, R. L., Arno, D. H., & Bachelder, R. L. *Summary of research and evaluation of the Youth Values Project, 1973-1976.* Mimeographed paper. Akron, Ohio, YMCA and National Board of YMCA's, 1976.

Gray, R. D., III. *The influence of values clarification strategies on student self-concept and sociometric structures in selected elementary school classrooms.* Unpublished doctoral dissertation, University of California, 1975.

Guziak, S. J. *The use of values clarification strategies with fifth grade students to investigate influence on self-concept and values.* Unpublished doctoral dissertation, Ohio State University, 1974.

Harmin, M., Kirschenbaum, H., & Simon, S. B. *Clarifying values through subject matter.* Minneapolis, Minn.: Winston Press, 1973.

Kaufman, M. A. *Comparison of a career course with individual counseling as facilitators of vocational development for college women.* Unpublished master's thesis, Cornell University, 1974.

Kelley, F. W. *Selected values clarification strategies and elementary school pupils' self concept, school sentiment and reading achievement.* Unpublished doctoral dissertation, Fordham University, 1976.

Kirschenbaum, H. *Recent research in values clarification.* Upper Jay, N.Y.: National Humanistic Education Center, 1974. Also in J. Meyer, B. Burnham, and J. Cholvat. *Values education.* Waterloo, Ontario: Wilfrid Laurier University Press, 1975.

Kirschenbaum, H., & Simon, S. B. (Eds.). *Readings in values clarification.* Minneapolis, Minn.: Winston Press, 1973.

Little, R. J. *A comparative study of the lecture approach and a values clarification approach to the teaching of driver education.* Brant County, Ontario: Board of Education, 1975.

Nowicki, S., & Strickland, B. R. A locus of control scale for children. *Journal of Consulting and Clinical Psychology*, 1973, *40*, 148–154.

Ojemann, R. H. *The meaning of casual orientation.* Preventative Psychiatry Research Program, State University of Iowa, 1961.

Osman, J. The use of selected value clarifying strategies in health education. *Journal of School Health*, 1974, *43*(10), 621–623.

Pracejus, E. *The effect of values clarification on reading comprehension.* Unpublished doctoral dissertation, University of Pittsburgh, 1975.

Quinn, R. E. Evaluation of a technique for clarifying environmental values with high school sophomores. *Dissertation Abstracts International*, 1970, *30*, 2875A.

Raduns, L. *The development of an instrument to measure value clarification in the area of ecology.* Unpublished master's thesis, University of Florida, 1973.

Raths, L. E., Harmin, M., & Simon, S. B. *Values and teaching.* Columbus, Ohio: Charles E. Merrill, 1966.

Redman, G. L. *An exploratory study of the effects of inservice value clarification training on openness of teacher assessing behavior.* Unpublished doctoral dissertation, University of Minnesota, 1975.

Rutkowski, D. M. *The use of values-clarification strategies in chemistry classes to develop positive attitudes toward science.* Unpublished master's thesis, State University College of New York at Oswego, 1975.

Simon, S. B., Howe, L. W., & Kirschenbaum, H. *Values clarification: A handbook of practical strategies for teachers and students.* New York: Hart, 1972.

Sklare, G. B. *The effects of the values clarification process upon the values, clarity of values and dogmatism of high school juniors and seniors.* Unpublished doctoral dissertation, Wayne State University, 1974.

Smith, B. C. Values clarification in drug education: A comparative study. *Journal of Drug Education*, 1973, *3*(4), 369–376.

Swift, M., & Spivack, G. *Revised DESB Scale.* Devon, Pa.: Devereux Foundation, 1974.

Warger, C. L. *Teacher attitudes in relation to using values clarification with mainstreamed emotionally impaired adolescents in the regular classroom and its implications.* Unpublished master's thesis, Eastern Michigan University, 1976.

Wenker-Konner, R., Hammond, E., & Egner, A. *A functional analysis of values clarification strategies on the participation rate of ten fifth graders.* Department of Special Education, University of Vermont, 1973.

Wilgoren, R. A. *The Relationship between the self-concept of pre-service teachers and two methods of teaching value clarification.* Unpublished doctoral dissertation, University of Massachusetts, 1973.

Chapter 4

SOME FREQUENTLY ASKED QUESTIONS ABOUT VALUE CLARIFICATION – AND SOME ANSWERS

The eighteen questions (and answers) that constitute this chapter are culled from the questions I am most frequently asked while giving speeches, workshops, or courses on value clarification. For some questions, both "shorter" and "longer" answers are indicated. For others I have given an answer and then an "addendum," another paragraph or more that may be added at the speaker's discretion. The appropriate length of any one answer will depend on several factors—time limits, audience interest, the speaker's comfort with the question, and his or her objectives for that session. Thus, the responses suggested below are meant to be adapted in terms of length and content to fit the particular context in which the questions are asked. (The whole issue of responding to questions is covered more fully in the discussion on general principles of designing and conducting value-clarification experiences in Chapter 5.)

I also want to emphasize that the answers below are *my* answers, and not necessarily the "right" answers to these questions. If some of the answers given here contain some ideas that other teachers or trainers may want to incorporate into their responses to questions on value clarification, then so much the better. But it is my hope that the reader will not commit these answers to memory, to recall and recite the next time one of these questions comes up. I would rather the reader mull these issues over and arrive at answers that are truly his or her own.

As many times as I have responded publicly to these questions, I still found it extremely helpful and a real learning experience to sit down and write out answers that I knew would be fixed permanently in print. I recommend this as a useful exercise for other teachers and trainers who wish to explore their own thinking on these issues and better prepare themselves to respond helpfully when questions arise.

HOW IS VALUE CLARIFICATION SIMILAR TO OR DIFFERENT FROM LAWRENCE KOHLBERG'S WORK?

This question can be presented in many different forms, but regardless of how the question is stated, the questioner undoubtedly has some familiarity with the work of Kohlberg or other developmental psychologists interested in the acquisition of moral reasoning. Kohlberg's six stages of moral development—making moral decisions on the basis of (1) avoiding punishment, (2) self-interest, (3) social acceptance, (4) rules and laws, (5) understanding the "social contract," and (6) devotion to higher principles—usually serves as the basis for most of the research conducted in this area. A whole chapter could be written just on the issues that the moral development school raises for value clarification, and vice versa.

Answer

Kohlberg and other moral developmentalists have focused exclusively on *moral* issues, questions involving "shoulds" and "oughts." Teachers of value clarification, on the other hand, have focused both on *value* issues ("How do you like to keep your room?") and on *moral* issues ("How do you think the United States should respond to the problem of world hunger?" "What are our alternatives?" "What are the consequences?" "What would you do if you were President?"). In addition, the moral developmentalists are interested exclusively in how to change people's moral *reasoning*, the way we think about moral dilemmas, and suggest that there is some correlation between moral reasoning and moral behavior. In contrast, value-clarification proponents focus directly on a wider range of human experience—the feeling realm, cognitive decision making, and observable behavior.

Both moral development and value clarification have avoided moralizing as an approach to education, and both place their faith in a *process*—the process of moral reasoning at the higher levels, or the valuing process. The values of justice, freedom, and equality are *explicit* in the higher stages of moral reasoning; the same values are *implicit* in the valuing process and the value-clarification methodology.

Although there has been no research to measure it, it may be hypothesized that value-clarification strategies, when used correctly, will help individuals move toward increasingly higher stages of moral reasoning. By the same token, the person operating at the fifth or sixth stage of Kohlberg's moral-development scale would likely be utilizing the valuing process.

Both approaches are consistent with the overall goal of helping individuals become more personally fulfilled and more constructive members of society. Though there are some differences between the two approaches, they can be integrated or used side by side to complement each other. Unfortunately, some developmentalists and some value clarifiers treat one another as enemies, which is absurd because both approaches grow out of the same democratic tradition and both have similar goals. Although their research orientations and methodologies may be somewhat different, these differences should be explored from a standpoint of common interest. It should be emphasized that the commonalities are much more significant than are the differences as far as the general public and the general education audience is concerned.

CAN HUMANS REALLY MAKE "FREE" CHOICES, OR IS ALL OUR BEHAVIOR DETERMINED BY PAST CONDITIONING?

Short Answer

Even when past conditioning influences us to behave in one way or another, if we can understand the forces that have conditioned us, if we can examine the social pressures around us, and we can look at the alternatives open to us then we are more capable of making a freer choice, a choice that is more our own and not just an echo of past conditioning and social pressures.

Longer Answer

There is nothing in the value-clarification theory that can solve, once and for all, the ancient debate about free will versus determinism. The best way to respond to this question is to explain what is meant by the valuing process of "free choice."

It is undeniable that all of us have been conditioned by our culture, our language patterns, our family, our peer group, our education, and countless other sources we may or may not be aware of. This lifelong conditioning process affects our thought patterns, our emotional reactions, and our behavior; in other words, our whole value orientation—what we think of as good and bad, what we feel attracted to or repelled by, and how we choose to live from moment to moment.

The Kwakiutal culture, which has been extensively described by anthropologists, (e.g., in Ruth Benedict's *Patterns of Culture*, 1934) has a value orientation that deems it desirable for a wealthy person periodically to burn all his precious possessions, to totally destroy his wealth; this is a sign of high status in the community. Other cultures, such as ours, regard it as desirable to accumulate wealth and pass it from generation to generation. Even within the same society, different conditioning processes are at work; for example, one social class may regard a given dress style as attractive and desirable, while another social class would regard the same style as ostentatious and in poor taste. So we are greatly affected by the value orientations of the different systems in which we are reared—and not only during our formative years. As adults, too, we move about in many social contexts, all of which exert some pressure on us to comply with the prevailing norms. And often those different pressures represent competing value orientations—church, business, family, peer group, etc.—all vying in varying degrees to influence our values. We never escape the conditions around us that tend to limit our alternatives and influence our choices by presenting certain consequences if we behave one way or another.

To acknowledge determinism, however, is not to deny choice. How we *perceive* our conditioning and how we perceive our alternatives and their consequences make an enormous difference in how we choose and how we act. If we believe we have no freedom, we act accordingly, as did those in the Nazi concentration camps who went passively to their deaths. On the other hand, if we believe that we *are* free, then we find alternatives, as did those in the same death camps who fought back, attempted escapes, prolonged their lives, or chose to die with dignity. If we perceive there are no alternatives ("The poor are always with us," "We are doomed to repeat the mistakes of history," "I'm basically a shy person," "You can't teach an old dog new tricks"), we go along as we always have. Once viable alternatives are perceived, it becomes possible to choose from among them, and we often do. Freedom is not, as Skinner (in *Beyond Freedom and Dignity*, 1971) suggests, only a meaningless carry-over from a romantic and liberal tradition. It is a real and measurable phenomenon. The more often people perceive alternatives and believe they are free, the more their observable, measurable behavior will be varied, creative, and productive. The experience of freedom is self-generating; the more often it is experienced, the more often it occurs.

Value-clarification activities help people discover and act upon the choices that exist for them by causing them to (1) examine the pressures around them, their past conditioning, and the roots of their value orientation; (2) weigh the pros and cons of present choices and consider new alternatives and their consequences; and (3) experience their own feelings about the alternatives and discover what they truly prize and cherish. To the extent that this process happens, the person becomes capable of making a "freer" choice. Value clarification helps us temporarily step out of the situation and decide how we will react, how we will re-enter the situation and behave. Perhaps we can never totally step so far back as to gain a total perspective—a complete understanding of our conditioning and the alternatives and consequences before us. In that sense, no choice can ever be totally free. But to the extent we can move in this direction, our choices become increasingly our own, increasingly free. (The meaning of free choice on a deeper psychological level is explored in the next question and answer.)

COULD A PERSON USE THE VALUING PROCESS AND BECOME A HITLER?

This question represents a classical test for the morality inherent in the valuing process, that is, whether the valuing process could be used toward immoral ends. In some ways, it calls into question the entire validity of value clarification, for if value clarification can make prejudice and inhumanity more likely to occur, I know of no one presently using the approach who would continue to do so. Thus, it seems undeniable that all value clarifiers believe implicitly or explicitly that the answer to this question is "no."

Short Answer

No. A psychologically disturbed person is severely hampered in his or her ability to make free choices and to rationally examine a wide range of alternatives and consequences. Hitler was clearly paranoid and could not effectively use the choosing processes of valuing.

Longer Answer

The conditioning process affects us on deep psychological levels as well as in ways that are more clearly observable. For instance, the way we are treated by significant others in our formative years, the type of nutrition we receive, the extent of fear, insecurity, embarrassment, frustration, loneliness, grief, physical and emotional hurt we experience, the amount of support and encouragement and acceptance we are surrounded with, all deeply influence the way in which we come to perceive ourselves, others, and life in general. Few if any of us escape without some scars—some residual hurt, fear, anxiety, or distress; some sense of being unlovable or unworthy at a basic level; or some feeling that we need to prove ourselves in order to feel worthwhile. *To the extent that we are in the grip of emotional distress, our capacity to think clearly and behave rationally diminishes* (Jackins, 1965). Probably all of us carry some of these scars around, and in subtle ways they limit our total effectiveness. But sometimes, early experiences are so severe that the scars that remain take the form of extreme psychological disturbance. In these instances, clinicians often attach such labels as paranoid, schizophrenic, catatonic, and the like.

Hitler, the prime example of totalitarian dictatorship, was such a person. All that we know of him suggests the psychological symptoms of paranoia. His illogical conclusions (e.g., "the Aryan race"), his scapegoating (e.g., Jews, Catholics, etc.), his lust for power (e.g., "tomorrow the world"), his repetitiveness, insistence on acquiescence, denial of his own background, and so on all characterize a person who is psychologically disturbed, incapable of rationally examining alternatives to his own position, and in the grip of compulsive behavior patterns. Clearly Hitler was not a model of the "valuing person."

But this is just one way to look at this question. Another way—one that does not require a belief in the psychological theory just expressed—goes beyond the single clinical example of Hitler. If there is a concern that helping people get in touch with what they prize and cherish and that helping them make free choices will increase the incidence of destructive behavior, let us turn to a group that has a great deal of experience dealing with people whose destructive behavior has gotten them into trouble or who are bordering on antisocial behavior. Clinical psychologists, therapists, and psychiatrists may represent many schools of thought, but all have one thing in common: If they were asked, "In your experience and from your research, if you help people become aware of their feelings so that they can discover what they truly prize and cherish, and if you help them rationally examine alternatives open to them and the consequences of these alternatives, and if they become more able to make free choices—that is, choices free from unconscious drives, compulsions, and rigid behavior patterns—would you say that those people are more or less likely to commit violence, steal, hurt others, behave irrationally, or run afoul of the law?" Almost unanimously, their answer would be *less likely*.

From everything we know about human behavior, the valuing process, if used consistently over time, will make it less likely that people will engage in destructive, antisocial behavior.

TO WHAT EXTENT SHOULD YOUNG CHILDREN BE ALLOWED TO EXERCISE FREE CHOICE? DOES VALUE CLARIFICATION ADVOCATE COMPLETE FREEDOM?

Answer

It seems to me that a major goal of education is to help people learn to use freedom responsibly. The infant has very little freedom; almost all things are decided for him. The adult is responsible for many free choices—in work, marriage, life style, politics, etc. We do not get from one place to the other all at once, but in stages. In structured situations, we can give children and teen-agers increasingly larger doses of freedom while we help them look at alternatives and consequences and utilize the other valuing processes. That is what value clarification and education is all about.

Addendum

Many people underestimate how much freedom a child can handle. I once asked a two-year-old girl if she preferred being called Cathy or Catherine. She was thinking about it when her mother answered for her. That two-year-old could have made that choice herself. Well-run open classrooms have illustrated that children can handle many choices about their education. As a teen-age scout leader, I was allowed to make just about every decision as to how twelve boys would eat, sleep, and spend their time for a four-day overnight hike. It is these kinds of responsibilities and opportunities for free choices that encourage the most rapid and significant learning. Children can handle a lot more than we usually give them credit for.

WHAT ABOUT DISCIPLINE? SUPPOSE A FIGHT BREAKS OUT? IS THAT THEIR FREE CHOICE TOO?

Answer

Not in my classroom. Nor is cheating, ridiculing others, or several other behaviors that are going to cause physical or emotional hurt and/or that can damage the climate of trust in our group. I put a stop to those right away. But I do not pretend that that is value clarification. It is discipline. And I do it to restore the climate in which value clarification can best occur—safety and trust.

Addendum

If two children are fighting, I do not go over and ask them whether they are proud of themselves or ask them to make a list of twenty alternatives to fighting. I simply stop the fight. I save value clarification for another time, when tempers are cooler, when reason is restored, and when they are not likely to think I am using value clarification to discipline them or to moralize to them.

That is what I do *when* problems occur, which they do from time to time. I want to emphasize that value clarification does not eliminate discipline problems; it just tends to reduce the frequency of their occurrence. Both teachers' reports and one careful research study (Wenker-Konner, Hammond, & Egner, 1973; see Chapter 3) indicate this.

WON'T TEACHERS' OWN BIASES CREEP IN, THEREBY IMPOSING THEIR VALUES ON THE STUDENTS?

Short Answer

To some extent this is inevitable. But if the teacher really wants the students to think for themselves, they will. In that context, an occasional lapse on the teacher's part will not seriously interfere with the goals of value clarification.

Longer Answer

First we must distinguish between the times a teacher publicly shares his or her values and those occasions when the teacher's values inadvertently or subtly influence his or her questions and responses to students.

In the first instance, it is completely legitimate for the teacher to share his or her views in a way that suggests "This is what *I* think; what do *you* think? I'd like to hear your ideas just as you listened to mine." As long as the teacher does not take too much air time, at the expense of giving the students a chance to think and speak for themselves, this type of sharing is not an imposition and, in fact, encourages the students to think for themselves through exposure to a good model of one who does.

The hidden intrusion of a teacher's values into a discussion is another matter, however. To some extent, it is inevitable, but the question is "To what extent?" If it happens all the time, the students will sense the imposition and will not participate except to curry the teacher's favor. This is not value clarification. On the other hand, if a teacher really does want students to think for themselves and usually treats a wide variety of viewpoints with respect, then an occasional lapse will not seriously interfere with the students' use of the valuing process. Teachers are human, and students know that (or at least suspect it).

TO WHAT EXTENT DOES PEER PRESSURE MAKE IT DIFFICULT FOR STUDENTS TO SAY WHAT THEY REALLY THINK AND FEEL?

Short Answer

Although peer pressure is usually present to some degree, the skillful teacher, when using value clarification, will minimize peer pressure on students' responses. Most students will respond honestly most of the time.

Longer Answer

The conformity engendered by peer pressure is one of the primary behaviors value clarification is designed to eliminate. Our goal is for students to think for themselves and be willing to express their views. If the teacher is skillful in using value clarification, peer pressure will have only a minimal influence on students' responses. Although it will usually be present to some small degree, most students will respond honestly most of the time.

There are many ways the facilitator learns to reduce peer pressure—introducing value clarification with low-risk topics on which peer pressure is not likely to operate; using other trust-building activities at the beginning of the year; stating that differences are to be expected; reinforcing the expression of minority viewpoints (not the viewpoint itself, but the fact that some were willing to express it); being a model of someone who is willing to stand up for minority viewpoints; introducing readings (e.g., Thoreau) or subjects (a scientist's determination to pursue his unique hypothesis) that present models of independent thinking and action; having students write down their answers before responding aloud; and so on. If peer pressure is still a big problem, the teacher can introduce it as a topic of discussion and clarification. This can be done indirectly (for example, by presenting a "value continuum" on "your willingness to be different," with "always agree" at one end and "never agree" at the other) or directly (for instance, by saying something like "I get the feeling that when we do value-clarification activities a lot of people are not willing to share their ideas because of the problem of pressure from others. It seems to me that if a lot of people are feeling that way it is going to interfere with what we are doing. Is my perception off? Do you see this as a problem too? What are your ideas on this?'").

In a small number of cases, peer pressure continues to operate a good deal of the time, despite the teacher's attempts to thwart it. Even so, students are probably benefiting from value clarification. Although they may not feel safe enough to express their views, most are at least thinking about them. In these instances, use more writing activities, give them the chance to share in smaller groups with people they trust (e.g., support groups), and then come back to large group sharing at a later time. But do not give up. If peer pressure cannot be licked right away, it can still be circumvented.

HOW DO YOU DEAL WITH THE "PUT-DOWNS" STUDENTS USE ON ONE ANOTHER?

Answer

"Put-downs," "killer statements," "insults,"—whatever you wish to call them—are one of the most insidious kinds of peer pressure operating inside or outside a classroom. Our culture is a "put-down culture." Count the number of put-downs you hear on television in an evening compared to the number of "validations" or statements of appreciation you hear. (This might make a good student activity.) Count the numbers of put-downs and validations at the family table. Count them in school, both from students and teachers. In any group put-downs reduce the level of trust and make it less likely students will speak their minds on controversial issues.

There are many ways to fight put-downs in a group setting. Some of these were mentioned in the response to the previous question; others might include some of the following:

1. Ignore an occasional put-down, especially if it does not seem to have hurt anyone's feelings and does not seem worth stopping an otherwise good discussion or activity to deal with.

2. Simply ask an individual or group to be quiet when you begin to hear the titters or words that indicate a put-down might be on the way.

3. Deal with those who tend to make "killer statements" individually and in positive ways; that is, recognize that a person puts someone else down in order to make himself or herself feel important and

find other ways to help the individual feel important—a public interview, validation, etc.

4. Declare a "moratorium" on "killer statements." Explain how
just as in the wild West the cowboys hung their guns on the saloon
door, in this group, we're going to hang our put-downs on the classroom
door, and why.

5. Do a value-clarification activity on the topic of put-downs. For
example, have the students make a list of twenty put-downs they know
of. Have them code their lists, using an "I" to signify "I've used this
put-down," a "ME" to indicate "it's been used on me," a star next to the
five that would bother them the most to hear, and so on. That should
start off an excellent discussion on the subject that is bound to sensitize
everyone to the problem. The class might then do a second activity
involving brainstorming possible solutions to the problem in their
class.

6. Confront the group directly: "I hear an awful lot of put-downs
when we do these kinds of activities. I don't know about you, but if I got
many of those comments directed at me, I'd think twice about opening
my mouth in this class, or saying what I really feel. Do *you* see it as a
problem? Or don't those statements and comments bother you?"

7. Tell the IALAC (I Am Lovable And Capable) story (Sidney
Simon, Argus, 1973). It can work wonders with a group.

8. Refer to Marianne Simon's article, "Chasing Killer Statements
from the Classroom," in the September, 1975 *Learning Magazine*. It
has several other good ideas to fight this unfortunate phenomenon.

IS IT APPROPRIATE FOR THE SCHOOLS EVEN TO BE INVOLVED IN THE TEACHING OF VALUES? ISN'T THAT THE REALM OF THE CHURCH AND THE HOME?

Answer

Value education is definitely the realm of the church and the home.
But the schools can play an important part too—not by teaching any
particular set of values, but by teaching the valuing and decision-
making skills students are going to need throughout their lives. These
skills include thinking for themselves, making responsible decisions
(i.e., choosing freely after weighing alternatives and consequences),
communicating their ideas and feelings, and acting upon their beliefs.
The school's job is to help educate responsible citizens of a democracy,
and these valuing skills are crucial toward that end.

HOW DO PARENTS REACT TO VALUE TEACHING IN SCHOOLS?

Short Answer

Many are indifferent, many are supportive, and a small minority are against it.

Longer Answer

Unfortunately, many are indifferent, just as they are about most things that schools do. But of those who care, most are supportive. Some parents are supportive because they understand the purposes of value clarification and agree with them; they are glad to have their children engaging in rational discussion with the diversity of viewpoints one finds in a typical classroom. Others do not know how to handle value issues, such as drugs and sexuality, in their own families and are relieved that someone else is doing something about it. Still others appreciate value clarification because their children report being more involved in and more positive toward school.

A minority of parents tend to oppose value clarification. They see it as a threat to their authority at home, which is partly true. A thinking person is always a threat to authoritarian leadership. In a larger sense, value clarification should pose no threat to parental authority, because, when it is done properly, it encourages more open and respectful communication within the family—despite the fact that there might be disagreements.

HOW DO YOU DEAL WITH THOSE PARENTS WHO OPPOSE VALUE CLARIFICATION? THEY CAN BE THE MOST VOCAL GROUP OF ALL.

Answer

Every community is different, but there are a few guidelines that may be useful to follow:

1. Do not introduce your value-clarification program with a lot of fanfare and publicity, but do make some announcement of it—in the school-parent newsletter, *as part of* a letter sent home with the children, as part of a PTA meeting, etc. Very briefly explain the program's goals and invite any interested parents to come in and learn more if they like.

2. In explaining value clarification to parents, either in a short newsletter announcement or in a lengthy meeting, emphasize the as-

pect of decision-making and communication skills and explain the valuing process. Parents recognize skill development as a legitimate function of the school. If asked, do not deny that religion, sexuality, and the family are occasionally discussed (if they are), but emphasize that these issues constitute a minor part of the program and that teachers are trying to help students develop their own values to live by, not trying to impose their own values on the students.

3. If a meeting with parents is held, involve them in a few carefully chosen strategies—20 Things You Love to Do, Proud Whip, etc.—that will gently introduce them to the techniques of value clarification.

4. If you are publishing a curriculum guide, avoid including any voting questions, rank orders, etc., that might be taken out of context and fan the flames of potential opposition.

5. If some parents strenuously object to value clarification and will not budge, provide an alternative learning experience for their children. Then go on to new problems and issues. Once you have tried to educate the community about value clarification and have provided an alternative option for children of those parents most opposed to it, do not encourage more controversy: there is nothing to be gained by prolonged argument.

6. Be aware of those content areas that are particularly volatile in your community. At times it might be best to avoid them entirely or to touch on them only lightly. If they are discussed in any depth, be certain to encourage and accept all viewpoints that may be present in the community. If any reading materials or handouts are used, be sure they are in good taste and represent balanced viewpoints. Remember that every rank order or continuum you use may get back to parents, usually out of context. So think carefully about every strategy you intend to employ.

7. On the most controversial issues, as far as the community is concerned, it may be best to withhold your own viewpoints, explaining your reasons for doing so to the students, if appropriate. They will understand. Nothing you have to say is so important that it is worth endangering the opportunity to have students share what *they* have to say.

8. You may want to encourage students to show their parents things they have written in response to selected value-clarification activities. One elementary teacher, for example, had her students take home the collages they made, which illustrated all the things they prized about their families.

These measures are not offered as a guarantee against parent/ community opposition, but they should make its occurrence less likely or briefer. (Another facet of community reaction to value clarification is discussed in Chapter 13.)

I TEACH GEOMETRY (OR BIOLOGY, ETC.): WHAT DOES VALUE CLARIFICATION HAVE TO DO WITH ME?

Answers to this type of question depend a great deal on how much time is available—and on whether and for how long the facilitator plans to work with the group on the three-levels approach to subject matter. (Teaching the three-levels theory is discussed in Chapter 9.) For instance, if I planned to deal with the three-levels approach later, I might give the first answer below.

Answer A

I would like to deal a little bit later with the question of how value clarification can be used with any and all subject areas. It is an important question that deserves some special attention, so if you don't mind waiting just a little while longer we will come back to that issue.

If I did not have the time or background to respond to such a question, I would refer the person to other resources, giving an answer such as the one below.

Answer B

I am sorry, but I do not have time to go into specific applications of value clarification to different subject areas now, but let me tell you where you can get some materials on applying value clarification to your subject. (Then I would mention *Clarifying Values Through Subject Matter* and other relevant articles and materials and make a materials list or bibliography available.)

Finally, if I had time and some specific ideas to offer, I would give some examples of how the three-levels approach might work in geometry (e.g., make a drawing of your ideal room, home, school, city, etc. using geometric shapes and measurements). But, again, I would emphasize how these few examples cannot do justice to the questioner's subject area, and I would give suggestions as to where he or she might go for further readings.

HOW CAN I MAKE TIME FOR VALUE CLARIFICATION? I HAVE SO MUCH TO COVER AND MY STUDENTS ARE REQUIRED TO TAKE STANDARDIZED ACHIEVEMENT TESTS.

Answer

No one can tell you how much time to spend on the fact, concept, or value levels of your subject. This is one of the most difficult choices you have to make as a teacher. But I can give you some comforting information. In almost every research study that measured subject matter comprehension in classes in which the value-clarification approach had been used, it was found that the value-clarification groups did *as well as or better than* the other groups on measures of knowledge and skill in the particular subject areas. (See Chapter 3 for research findings on this issue.)

I TRIED SUCH AND SUCH A STRATEGY AND IT DIDN'T WORK.

Sometimes this is followed by a question, like "What did I do wrong?" Sometimes it is a simple declarative statement, sometimes a challenge to the validity of what you are trying to present. Such a question offers both a trap and an opportunity for the group leader. The trap is hidden in the temptation to diagnose the problem and offer a solution, even though the questioner may not really be asking for alternatives. So if you make a suggestion and then the questioner says, "I tried that, it didn't work," it is easy to spend ten minutes trying to understand and solve one person's problem at the expense of the whole group. The answer given below is one way to forestall that possibility.

Answer

There might be any number of reasons it did not work. Why don't you see me during the break (or after the session, etc.) and we will see if we can figure out what went wrong. (Of course, saying this implies a willingness to follow through with some exploration of the questioner's problem.)

On other occasions, when I think I have an accurate sense of the problem, and when I think I have something worthwhile to say, I share the insights, suggestions, or concerns I have that could not only help the questioner but also inform the entire group. On still other occasions, I might invite participants to share their ideas on the problem. Again, I would avoid the type of discussion that encourages group members to start throwing out ideas, if they cause the original questioner to become defensive.

IS THERE ANY RESEARCH TO SUPPORT VALUE CLARIFICATION? ARE THERE ANY GOOD INSTRUMENTS YOU COULD RECOMMEND TO ME?

Answer

The first part of that question is easier to answer than the second.

Yes, there is a growing body of data, over thirty studies, that indicate that value clarification can reduce apathy, enhance self-esteem, reduce drug abuse, and contribute to other laudable goals, while simultaneously enabling the student to maintain or increase her learning capacity in terms of cognitive skills and school subject matter. Although these conclusions must be held very tentatively, pending further research, the direction of the present findings is clear. For a further look into the existing research, I recommend the research chapter in *Values and Teaching* (1966), and Chapter 3 of this text.

In answer to the question of whether there is an instrument to measure the effectiveness of value clarification, the answer is that it depends on what you consider effective; that is, what you want to measure. I know of no instrument that directly measures the use of the whole valuing process. A paper-and-pencil or observational tool that could distinguish someone who skillfully and frequently uses the valuing process (a "high-valuing" person) from someone who does not (a "low-valuing" person) would be a great contribution. But currently we have only approximations of such an instrument (Louis Raths' early evaluation approach described in *Values and Teaching;* the Wenker-Konner observation tool) or instruments that measure only one dimension or one subprocess within the valuing process.

If, on the other hand, there is a specific goal—such as reducing vandalism, increasing attendance, enhancing self-esteem, reducing illegal drug use, moving to higher stages of moral reasoning, enhancing school achievement, and so on—there are valid and reliable ways in which to measure the results of value clarification. Some of the specific instruments are mentioned in the two research sources referred to earlier.

WHERE CAN I FIND MATERIALS ON VALUE CLARIFICATION? MOST BOOKSTORES DON'T CARRY THEM.

Answer

I have a stack of flyers here with a list of materials that can be ordered from the National Humanistic Education Center. (On the other side is a listing of introductory and advanced value-clarification workshops offered around the country.) I'll leave them on this table; help yourself if you'd like to take one. Some other resources I know of are ―――――――― (mention local programs, organizations, etc.).

HOW DOES VALUE CLARIFICATION RESPOND TO BEHAVIORAL OBJECTIVES AND ACCOUNTABILITY?

Answer

Any educator should be able to explain what his or her goals are and have some evidence to indicate that those goals are being accomplished to a reasonable degree. The objectives of the value clarifier should be clear. The most important and inclusive objective, stated in strict behavioral terms, might be: *When confronted by an important decision, the student will select and skillfully utilize the appropriate valuing processes. The processes chosen will meet the criteria of "appropriate selection" and "skillful utilization" if the actual consequences of these processes are both personally satisfying and socially constructive* (see Chapter 1 for a definition of the latter).

The problem with broad objectives like this is that they are almost impossible to measure. So, instead, we cut them down to a more workable size; we break the objective down into bite-size chunks. For example:

Given a value dilemma requiring a decision, the student will be able to think of four realistic alternatives that might be followed.

Each Monday, the student will be able to report one thing he or she is proud of having done the previous week.

It could be done. With ingenious instruments, students could be measured on their use of the valuing process. If this is done occasionally, for the purpose of diagnosis, teacher feedback, or evaluating the success of a value-clarification program or course, then some purposes, including accountability, may be served.

But the implementer of such an instrument must be careful to avoid abusing it. Diagnosis may soon turn to regular testing, and shortly thereafter, to grading. "Johnny is underachieving in 'prizing,' but slightly ahead of grade level in 'choosing.' " The moment students begin to feel graded—literally or emotionally—the potential benefits of this design will remain unrealized. Value clarification will have become as aversive as most other school subjects: students may use the valuing process scrupulously while in class and while completing their homework assignments—much as they now (some of them) write compositions and answer the questions at the end of the chapter. And then they will promptly forget it all, or most of it, and go about their value-conflicted business as usual.

A value-clarification curriculum *should* be held accountable for achieving its objectives. But any measuring of this achievement must be very sparing and unobtrusive, lest the testing procedure thwart the educational goals.

REFERENCES

Benedict, R. *Patterns of culture*. Boston: Houghton-Mifflin, 1934.

Jackins, H. *The human side of human beings*. Seattle, Wash.: Rational Island Publishers, 1965.

Raths, L. E., Harmin, M., & Simon, S. B. *Values and teaching*. Columbus, Ohio: Charles E. Merrill, 1966.

Skinner, B. F. *Beyond freedom and dignity*. New York: Knopf, 1971.

PART II:

DESIGNING VALUE-CLARIFICATION EXPERIENCES

Chapter 5

DESIGNING VALUE-CLARIFICATION EXPERIENCES: GENERAL PRINCIPLES

Value-clarification proponents have always tried to communicate to teachers and others that there is no right way to use the value-clarification approach, and this message may be applied equally to value-clarification training. There is no one right way to design a value-clarification workshop, course, or unit. All of us have our own style, favorite strategies, weak areas, priorities, and experiences with other methods and approaches that we bring to our value-clarification training programs. For instance, I have often witnessed a co-leader of mine doing something with the group that made me groan inwardly with the feeling that it would never work or that we had lost the participants' interest. But more often than not it turned out fine. Some strategies or designs I simply cannot pull off effectively, but my colleague can, and vice versa. The issue, then, is not "Do you have the right design?" but "Can you make it work?" It almost seems that I could take my carefully worked out, two-day workshop design and reverse the entire order—doing the last strategy first (IALAC), the first last (Value Name Tags), and so on—and still make it work; that is, still reach my objectives, which are enumerated at the end of this chapter.

Having said this, it may seem contradictory to proceed with a chapter devoted to generalizations about effective workshop designs. However, while there may be many "right ways" to accomplish something, there can also be several "wrong ways," that is, ways that experience has shown often produce undesired results. The following principles, then, are introduced to warn the reader against some common pitfalls. This is not to say that violating any one of these guidelines will automatically doom a workshop or class to failure. The value-clarification approach is credible enough on its own merits to allow facilitators the leeway to make some mistakes and still be successful.

63

Up to a point. To avoid reaching that point, it would be wise to keep the following proven principles in mind when designing and executing value-clarification experiences.

EXPERIENTIAL FOCUS

Most people come to value-clarification workshops for specific practical strategies they can use in their classes, jobs, or homes, and/or to participate in a personal growth experience. Both purposes suggest an experiential design.

The best way to teach the strategies is to have people experience them. Clearly, this is true for my own learning. Someone can describe a new activity to me in detail. I can picture it, I can think, "That's really a good one, it would work very well," but only one in fifty times will I ever actually use it. On the other hand, when I *experience* a strategy, I feel its impact directly, it becomes a part of me, fixed in my memory, I get some insight about how to explain the directions clearly and about the timing. Assuming my experience with the strategy was a good one, I am motivated to use it with others. This is true for most people. The old proverb "There's no substitute for experience" aptly applies.

For this reason, the greater part of a value-clarification workshop should be experiential. Individually, in small groups, or in the whole group, participants should explore their own values, make up rank orders, practice new skills, and, in general, participate actively in the learning experience. This does not mean the facilitator should avoid theoretical input (an earlier chapter underlined the importance of teaching the value-clarification theory); it does mean that the balance should be carefully considered. In my workshops, 20 to 30 percent of the time is spent on theoretical input, and 70 to 80 percent on experiences or demonstrations with participants. I would hold to this even in an hour-long presentation, in which I take fifteen to twenty minutes to explain the value-clarification theory and forty to forty-five minutes to demonstrate value-clarification strategies with a small group of students, teachers, or audience members.

Sometimes a trainer goes into a workshop with all good intentions of having a balance of theory and experience. He begins with a twenty-minute lecture, then entertains a few questions. Perhaps the third question is a bit tricky and requires a longer answer. A person in the back of the room objects to something that was said. Someone else wants to comment on that. The trainer responds. Before long, fifty minutes have passed, with 90 percent of the group having listened passively the whole time. Worse yet, the trainer, fifty minutes earlier, had just promised them an experiential workshop. Trust and energy levels are falling. The trainer's good intentions have come to naught—which leads us right into the next point.

KEEP LECTURES SHORT

People can only process and remember a limited amount at one time. My colleague Merrill Harmin says, "Anything worth saying can be said in fifteen minutes" or "Anything that can't be said in fifteen minutes should be saved for another time." I would not go so far, but the point is a good one. I usually give one half-hour lecture and several ten to twenty minute "lecturettes" during a two-day workshop. Still, this is something I need to be continually vigilant about. More often than I like, I sense that I took twenty minutes to say something I could have said in fifteen, or four minutes to say what I could have said in two.

Most people who attend value-clarification workshops have been brought up on long lectures and lots of note-taking. Yet, once we create an expectation that this experience is going to be different, there is a certain kind of anticipation that leads to disappointment if this promise is not fulfilled. So if the participants have been involved in engaging conversation about a value-clarification exercise, it is more difficult for them to become passive listeners than if they expected from the start to play a passive role.

There is nothing wrong with a long lecture per se. If the participants expect it and if I am a good speaker with a well-organized and substantive message to deliver, there is no reason why the audience and I cannot spend a productive hour or more that way. But in the context of a value-clarification workshop, long lectures (and question and answer exchanges) tend to work against the sense of community, sharing, and personal exploration we are trying to create.

LOW-THREAT BEGINNING

Many people come into a new group slightly frightened or anxious, ready to risk a bit but not sure how safe it is. Our job is to make it safe, so people can try new behaviors and share their thoughts and feelings when they are ready. Thus, if we have people do Value Name Tags (#19) at the beginning, we ask, "Where is a place you would like to spend a year's vacation?" rather than "Write down a sentence you would like to tell your spouse or best friend, but never have." We ask questions that emphasize the positive—goals, high points, good memories, strong values, loved ones, and so on. These questions and topics create a feeling of acceptance and support—the best foundation for tackling the difficult value issues that will be dealt with later. Pointing out early in the workshop that participants have the right to pass on a question or activity is another way of lowering the threat level.

Certain topics may be more threatening in some groups than in others. For example, if I were working with a group of Boston school teachers in the summer of 1976 and began with a simple voting question, such as "How many of you favor busing?" I might suddenly find people looking at each other suspiciously, feeling defensive, being reminded of recent arguments they had been involved in, and feeling that this was a threatening situation. In other words, I have found it is important to be aware of the nature of, and the issues important to, the group, with whom I am working. Low threat allows people to be open to new alternatives and to give value clarification a fair chance. High threat creates a need for people to solidify previous positions, thereby thwarting the possibility of achieving personal or professional growth.

ATTENTION TO DETAIL

One of my earliest learnings as a teacher of value clarification, with Sid Simon and Merrill Harmin, was the necessity for extreme attention to details when planning a value-clarification workshop. There are almost endless questions that need answers. Do you divide group members into subgroups and then give them instructions, or do you first give the instructions and then divide people into subgroups? Do you present two or three sample Rank Orders? In moving from the first sharing trio to the next one, do you have members number off, one, two, and three, and have the One's stay seated and the Twos and Threes get up and find new partners by sitting down next to Ones, or do you have all of them stand up and find new partners? Does the co-leader take over during the name-tag, milling-around time, or does the primary leader get members into trios and then have the co-leader take over? Is enough newsprint up on the wall to begin with, so you will not have to scurry around for newsprint and tape in the middle of a sequence? Do you distribute the handout while members are finishing up the last strategy and thus save time, or do you hold it until they are done so as not to distract them? Do you allow two minutes or three minutes for this focus group? And on and on.

To a first-time participant in a value-clarification workshop, the procedure often looks deceptively simple. Behind the scenes, there are dozens of minute decisions that must be made. The more experience one has, or the more one works with the same team-teacher, the less time these decisions occupy, but they are always there.

Although a workshop will not succeed or fail on the basis of any one or several of these separate decisions, the cumulative effect of these many choices can mean the difference between a fair workshop or a good one, a good one or an excellent one, and so on. It is well worth the time to plan carefully, paying lots of attention to detail.

AVOID MORALIZING OR DEFENDING

A workshop leader may be quite ready to accept all views offered on the topics of politics, religion, money, etc., but be unable to avoid moralizing on the subjects of education or value clarification. For example, "You *should* be doing value clarification," "If you moralize to students you are really hurting them," "Unless you publicly affirm your belief, you do not really believe it," and so on. It is rarely that blatant, but the tone comes across.

First of all, statements like these are rarely true. Maybe not all teachers *should* use value clarification; some teachers do other things more effectively. As long as students learn the valuing process, why must all teachers employ it? Maybe moralizing does not always hurt—it does not teach the valuing process, but to some students, moralizing at least means somebody cares about them. And, of course, it is entirely possible to sincerely believe in something without publicly affirming it. All things being equal, the beliefs one chooses to publicly affirm are probably *stronger* beliefs than those one never happens to mention, but even this is not always so. We tread on dangerous ground when we begin to moralize. We risk turning off teachers and professionals by moralizing as much as we do to adolescents. And when participants feel criticized or attacked, they return the favor. Then we get defensive, and instead of working toward a common goal we and the participants are in a power struggle.

The tone I find helpful is "Sure there are lots of ways of dealing with values, and each has its pros and cons (including value clarification). Value clarification seems most effective in teaching the valuing process. If we want to teach the valuing process, here are some ways it can be done. If we moralize to students, then we stop giving them practice using that process." For me, the most gratification comes from facilitating the valuing process while simultaneously modeling my values and sharing them with students at appropriate times in the discussion. In this way I can avoid a defensive posture and make our work together a matter of my sharing with the students some techniques and ideas that have been helpful in achieving our common goal—learning the valuing process.

VARY THE GROUP DYNAMICS

In any workshop that lasts more than a couple of hours, it is important to vary the nature of the group process. The group dynamic operates in many different ways depending on whether people are sitting and listening; participating as a whole group; working in sextets, trios, or individually; and so on. It is also a different process when people are talking as opposed to writing, or moving about the room as opposed to sitting in one place.

One of the advantages to the array of value-clarification strategies is that the group leader can select them to vary the ways in which the group interacts. If, on the other hand, I were to utilize one strategy after another, all of which employ a trio structure, two things would occur: first, I would give the erroneous impression that value clarification is almost always done in trios, and second, I would start to bore the group—people's energy levels would subside and less learning would take place. So in planning a workshop with a team-teacher, one or the other of us will frequently stop to think about what dynamics we will be creating as a result of the techniques we are planning to use. For example, "They will have been sitting for forty minutes straight, how about something like the Either-Or strategy (#5), which will get them moving around," or "So far everything we've done has involved people thinking off the top of their heads and then sharing with others; let's do something more reflective, using pencil and paper, and alone time," or "All our small-group work has been in quartets; let's do some trios or pairs, so as not to give the impression that quartets are the best groupings to use," and so on. The principle is to vary the nature of group interaction so as to better illustrate the possible uses of value clarification and to keep the workshop more interesting and the energy level higher.

TIMING

I find it important to work out my time schedule ahead of time. In our joint planning sessions, for example, my co-leader and I might write down something like the following for an afternoon during a two-day workshop:

1:00—Singing
1:15—Questions and Answers
1:30—Voting, Ranking, and Continuum, in sextets
2:00—Practice Session—trios
2:20—Practice Session—sextets
2:45—Break
3:00—Public Interview
3:15—Group Interview
3:30—Group Interview Practice
4:00—Finish ("I Wonder Statements," if time)

Part of our planning involves discussing whether our time allotments are realistic. Even when we agree on a time schedule, it is often difficult to stick to it. But doing this preparation increases the likelihood that we will accomplish our objectives. The time limits in the subsequent chapters may seem arbitrary, but they are based on experience with using that particular design. This does not mean that the same time limits for the same design will work for all facilitators. Each of us has different pace preferences and different styles. We have to discover our own time limits for the various designs we employ. The principle I am stressing here is not to be lazy about the preparation: It is important each and every time we design a value-clarification experience.

POST A RUNNING LIST OF STRATEGIES

I have found it very helpful to post, in a conspicuous location, a list of the strategies as they are introduced. In this way, participants have a continual reminder that we are not doing these things just for our own amusement, but that each is a distinct teaching method, with specific objectives and its own proper form of execution. Participants are reminded that they can use each of these strategies in their own back-home settings. Even if they do not take notes during the workshop, they are likely to copy down this list of strategies before they leave.

FORM GROUPS BEFORE GIVING INSTRUCTIONS

As a rule, I find it better to ask people to get into pairs, trios, or whatever, first, and then give them the instructions for the activity.

Although this procedure adds to the number of times I have to interrupt them to give instructions, it seems better than the alternative, which would be to give instructions, ask them to form small groups, and then have them forget the instructions during the process of forming the groups. In a workshop, I probably follow this guideline 80 percent of the time.

BE CLEAR ABOUT OBJECTIVES AND STRIVE TO ACCOMPLISH THEM

This is probably implied in many of the previous sections of this chapter; but since writing the foregoing last week, I attended a conference that made me want to add this section. It was a conference on teaching about world hunger. I attended as a participant. After the opening speech, the next three sessions were designed to be of practical help to educators. All three foundered because the leaders either were not clear about their objectives or did not take the necessary steps to accomplish them.

Two of the sessions made the same mistake. The leaders had some fine teaching materials to distribute to the group and one of them wanted to involve us in a simulation exercise about world hunger. But, after hearing the moving keynote address, they just could not resist making a few points of their own about world hunger. Actually, they were both well informed and what they had to say was interesting. And because it was interesting, some of the participants in the group wanted to ask questions or add some of the things *they* knew about world hunger. Before long the time was almost gone, both leaders recognized their plight and hurriedly began to distribute the materials or begin the simulation. The first had barely enough time to hand the materials out, and the second took us only ten minutes into an hour-long simulation.

I wonder if they were really clear about their objectives. They must have been, to some extent, because the sessions were advertised as practical how-to-do-it type sessions and they each began by saying they wanted to "demonstrate," "show us," etc. There are many possible explanations for why they got thrown off the track. One I want to mention is what I think of as a mistaken conception of democracy/or student involvement. We have been taught in many ways that it is desirable to have students involved, asking questions, sharing their thoughts and information and feelings. Clearly, value-clarification strategies are meant to maximize student involvement. But there are also times when it is appropriate to say "Please hold your questions or comments for later. If we're going to get through with this, we have to keep on going." Some leaders seem unable to resist the invitation of a raised hand, no matter what the consequences. For example, at the conference, the program chairperson had just informed one of these two leaders that time had just about run out and he should get on with passing out his materials. So he finished the point he was making and began to apologize to the two or three people who had their hands raised, when the same program chairperson broke in and said "Oh, well, I guess we can make time for a few more questions." And there were three more panel members waiting their turns!

The third "practical" session at the conference was, of all things, a three-level value clarification approach (facts, concepts, and values) to teaching about hunger.

They began to explain the three-levels theory, doing a very good job on the first two levels. When they got to the values level, they became rather abstract. Instead of giving specific examples of what questions teachers could ask students or what activities could be done on the values level, they hinted about this possibility in more general terms. I understood what they meant and agreed 100 percent. But the teachers were getting lost and getting a bit turned off. The leaders had an excellent grasp of value clarification and were clearly deeply committed to it. But they were starting to come across as ivory tower academics, a sure way to alienate classroom teachers. Again, they were defeating their objective.

Then, as an example of what students could do on the values level, they began discussing a technical solution to financing the alleviation of world hunger—a solution that some of their students had come up with. They described their alternative in great detail. One minute into their solution, and the audience had lost the point (never made very clearly to begin with) that this was what *students* could be doing on the values level—generating their own alternatives and acting on them. As it turned out, their alternative was not very popular with the group, and argument began to wage hot and heavy about its merits. Soon their particular solution was confused with value clarification, and value clarification fell under attack as Skinnerian, indoctrinating, and many other things I shudder to recall. Why did they have to give that example? They realized themselves what had happened, but by then it was too late; they were defending the example. Again, lack of clarity about objectives and inappropriate means for achieving them brought on self-defeat.

I once knew an English department chairman who used to say, "If you want to teach about jockey shorts and the best way to do it is to drop your trousers, then go ahead and do it." I don't think he meant it literally (though we sometimes had our doubts), but the point is a good one: to have confidence in our objectives and to do what is necessary to accomplish them. My objectives in designing value-clarification training experiences—short ones or long ones—are almost always the same: (1) the participants will leave with a positive attitude toward value clarification, including a desire to apply it in their back-home setting; (2) the participants will leave with a basically sound understanding (even if an introductory one) of what value clarification is and of how some of the strategies work; and (3) the participants will try some of the strategies in their classes, homes, or other settings. And, for longer workshops, in which participants have time to become more deeply involved in some of the strategies, I have a fourth objective: (4) the participants will experience some personal value clarification. This is valuable for its own sake and also contributes to the other three objectives. My own experience has shown, and a few research studies have verified, that if the above objectives are met, participants who go back home and try out the strategies are usually successful in their attempts. The reinforcement they receive from their students, children, clients, etc., then starts a cycle of continual further involvement in and understanding and utilization of value clarification and humanistic education.

These four objectives for value-clarification training help clarify many decisions I make about workshop designs. The following two chapters in this section describe some different designs that I have used for various types of workshops. Any workshop can be designed in many different ways, and quite a few of those ways can help participants to learn and experience the valuing process. The designs in the following chapters are presented not as models for the reader to replicate, but to illustrate how workshop content, program objectives, and design principles are filtered through the facilitator's own *style* of teaching and training. The examples reveal my experience, my biases, my special concerns, and my style. They show what goes on inside me as I plan a program and respond to the needs and interests of participants.

Chapter 6

DESIGN FOR A TWO-DAY WORKSHOP

What follows is a design I have used many times in two-day value-clarification workshops. More particularly, this design is for a weekend workshop—9 A.M. to 4 P.M. on Saturday; 9 A.M. to 3:30 P.M. on Sunday—that the participants have chosen to attend and for which many are paying themselves. The participants represent many different backgrounds; most are teachers, but some are administrators, social workers, counselors, nurses, students, parents, and so on. I have used this design, or one like it, with groups as small as thirty members and as large as three hundred members (but for the latter I worked with a partner and only attempted it after I had had a good deal of experience working with smaller groups). These details are important because the workshop design should be adjusted if either the timing of the workshop or the composition of the group is different.

This chapter is written in the first person singular, not because I am always the sole workshop leader—many times I work together with a team-teacher—but for the sake of simplicity. If I work with another person, we alternate leading different parts of the workshop.

FIRST MORNING

Starting on Time

This point is very important to me (although I have worked with colleagues who were less anxious about it than I) for two reasons. First, two days is never enough to accomplish what I want to in a workshop (neither is a week or two weeks, it seems), and starting ten minutes late wastes ten valuable minutes. It actually wastes more, because once the precedent is set, people are likely to come strolling in late after lunch and again the next day, confident that we will not be starting on time. If you figure ten minutes each for the two mornings, two breaks, and two lunches, a whole hour out of an eleven- or twelve-hour workshop is wasted. Second, some people are even more anxious about time than I am. A late start gets them angry. Why antagonize a few people first thing in the morning?

On the other hand, I would not carry this point to an extreme. If unusual weather conditions or bad directions to the workshop site or some other factor results in only half the people being there at 9:00 A.M., then I would be defeating my own purposes to begin on time. In that case, I explain the problem and announce a new starting time to the group already assembled.

Comfort and Caring

I always take a little time at the beginning of the workshop to help people be a bit more comfortable about the setting and to begin establishing a caring climate in the group. This might include a warm welcome; going over the meeting times; seeing whether everyone has a place to stay that night or needs help finding a ride home; asking if anybody has any questions about any of these kinds of details before we get started; briefly mentioning the purposes of the workshop— professional and personal; finding out by a show of hands where people are from and what their professions or grade levels are.

One's attitude in this opening period is very important. If I go through these details the way a teacher would make the morning announcements at school, or like an airline flight attendant explaining how to use oxygen masks, or if I have an attitude that I read somewhere I am supposed to have to make these announcements (which I do not really think are important), then people will not feel comfortable or cared about and the purpose is defeated at the outset. But if my attitude is friendly and I communicate the sense that I am there not just to teach them something but also because I care about them and would like each person in the group to be able to relax, feel truly a part of the proceedings, and know that this is a group in which people will help one another, then people are going to be much more ready and willing to participate actively in what lies ahead.

Value Name Tags (#19)

Most of the strategies I mention here are described in *Values Clarification: A Handbook of Practical Strategies* (Simon, Howe, & Kirschenbaum, 1972). Since that source describes in detail the strategies, their purpose, and how to use them, I will not repeat that material here. What I want to show is how these strategies work within an overall design.

First, I make certain that all participants receive 5″ X 8″ index cards prior to the beginning of the workshop. These cards are then converted into name tags by having people write their first names in big letters in the middle of the cards. The point is for others to be able to see their names from across the room and call them by name.

The participants then remove their name tags and I ask them to respond to several questions by writing the answers on their tags. I make sure they know they will be putting these back on, so if there is anything they do not want known about themselves, they can choose not to answer the question or they can write it on the back rather than front of the tag. One thing I like to ask them to do is to write down two values that are very important to them. I tell them not to ask me what I mean by "values," that we will come back to that later, but that they should respond according to whatever the word means to them. When I have asked them for all the information I want, I ask them to put their name tags back on. (I make a name tag for myself in the same way.)

Milling

I ask participants, with their name tags on, to mill randomly about the room looking at one another's name tags, eyes, shoes, faces, or whatever. I impose only one rule—no talking. I make sure to state that rule a couple of different ways before they stand up so I do not have to hush them to be quiet. (Of course, I also mill around as part of the group.) I let this go on for about five minutes, long enough for people to stop in front of about ten others and read their tags. Then I ask people to stop right where they are and look around at the group—observing the people they "met" and those who are still total strangers, people they think they will have a lot in common with, and people they think they could get into a good argument with (long pauses, to allow them time to look around). Then I ask them to choose two other people they do not know and sit down together in a comfortable spot. I remain aware of the groups and call out, "Are there any two's looking for one?" "They need one person back there," or whatever seems appropriate.

Sharing Trios (#20)

At this point I give about three minutes of theory input relating to risk—how we grow by taking risks and how each person should be allowed to set his or her own risk level by retaining the right to pass on a question or to say as much or as little as desired. I explain how each person will have two or three minutes to talk to the other two people about a topic I will suggest. Without going into a long explanation of the Focus Game strategy (#18), I do remind them to focus, that is, to give the person who is speaking their full attention, without interrupting, for a full two minutes. Then I ask my first question, "What is something you are proud of (I explain what I mean by 'proud') in one of the two following areas: (1) in relation to your work, or (2) in relation to the topic of love and/or sex?" (I keep track of the time from the front of the group.)

Once all three people in each group have had a chance to speak, I form new groups. I like the method of having them number off one–two–three in each group. I ask them, "When it comes to picking and choosing groups, are you more of a pick*er* or a pick*ee*?" and I explain how the picker is the more aggressive, the pickee the more passive, how neither style is "correct," how we are sometimes different in different settings, how we usually have a predominant style, and how this workshop affords the opportunity to try a different style to see what it is like, and so on. Then I explain how the number Ones will be automatic pickees and will sit where they are with one finger held high. The Twos and Threes will stand and separate. The Twos will go off in search of another Three, and the Threes will go off in search of another Two. When and only when they find each other will they sit down next to a new number One. Again, I emphasize that, if possible, they should find people they do not already know, explaining how they will have plenty of time later to talk with the people they know; that the workshop affords a unique opportunity to meet new people; and so forth. I have gone into detail in explaining the group movement method to reinforce the idea of the careful attention to detail used in the workshop. This same set of directions, said unclearly, can lose several valuable minutes and leave people feeling as though they did not do it right, or that I messed them up.

On the next sharing trio, I ask participants to close their eyes and think of a time they had an important decision to make, maybe long ago or recently or even right now. I ask them to recall the alternatives they were considering, the pros and cons they were weighing, whether anyone was helpful or not helpful to them in their decision making, and, if it was a past decision, what they chose and how it worked out, or, if it is a present decision, which way they are leaning and how they think it will work out. Then I ask them to open their eyes and share part or all of their story with the two others in their trio. Again, I keep time. At the end of this trio, I may explain the notion and strategy of Unfinished Business (#46).

For the third trio, I ask them to look down at the two "values" they wrote on their name tags. I ask them, "What do you actually *do* in your life to indicate that this is a value of yours? How is your behavior different from what it would be without that value?" And I give them an example of what I mean by talking about what *I* do about one of the values on *my* name tag.

By the end of this session, the three sharing trios have had a question related to prizing, choosing, and acting—three dimensions of the valuing process.

Break

Here I announce a ten-minute break and, after eight minutes, start gathering them back. I may be talking to one or more participants during the break, but I am careful not to allow this to interrupt the schedule.

Theory

At this point I like to explain a little of the value-clarification theory. Some trainers prefer to wait until the afternoon, or even the second day, when the participants have experienced more of the strategies. Frankly, my decision is based as much on what makes *me* feel comfortable as it is on my sense of the group. I am uncomfortable until I present the theory. I imagine that many of the participants are sitting there thinking, "Well, all these games are very nice, but what's the point of it? Why are we doing this?" I recognize that this is bothering only a minority, maybe even a very small minority of the members; still, I do not feel comfortable. I need to set the workshop in perspective fairly early in the proceedings. In addition to providing comfort for that minority and me, I think it helps everyone to understand each strategy in light of the valuing process. On the other hand, I would not want to introduce much theory *too early* in the workshop. That would set a typical teacher-talk-and-student-be-passive norm and make it more difficult for participants to become actively involved later. It is a balance I want, and doing the theory at this point seems about right for me.

In a previous chapter, I discussed several ways to teach the value-clarification theory. At this point, in this type of workshop, I prefer a straightforward lecture. I allow up to half an hour, even though that may be stretching the limits of the participants' listening attention, given what has come before. So, if I talk for the full half hour, I ask people to save their questions until a bit later. If I talk for twenty minutes, I might take up to about ten minutes of questions or comments.

In that half hour, I refer to the areas of confusion and conflict in values (on a prepared chart), I discuss different ways of helping people with value confusion or lack of values, I describe the valuing process, and I outline the four ways value clarification attempts to teach the valuing process. With practice, I can make almost every word count and thereby keep to the allotted time. I would rather see someone divide the lecture into two halves, to be presented at different times during that first day, than to turn an exciting theory into a long and tedious lecture.

Twenty Things

Twenty Things You Love To Do (#1) is especially appropriate at this point. It illustrates beautifully the value theory just presented.

One problem with using this strategy is that so many people have already done it. When I ask a group how many people have used this, anywhere from none to all of the participants raise their hands, depending on which trainers they have worked with, what college courses they have taken, and so on. If more than a handful are already familiar with this strategy, I provide two sets of directions. I do the regular strategy with the "newcomers," and I have the "old-timers" do a different inventory, with a different set of codings. Some of these variations might include the following: twenty things you would love to do before you die; think of someone you love and list twenty things you love to do with that person; twenty places you love to go; twenty things you love (like) about your work; and so on.

I try to help participants think of as many things they love as possible. I do not care if they have less than twenty items, but because it feels good to see a long list of "loves" before you and because the more they have the more they will have to work with on the coding, after they have worked for a while, I ask them to think of seasons of the year or places or people they love, because these things often stimulate new items for them to record. I make a list, too, on the chalkboard or on a chart so that the participants know I am participating, but I scrawl the items illegibly to protect my privacy. Other facilitators choose to write their lists quite legibly; again, we are all different. It is important that as teachers and trainers we know our own limits and protect ourselves accordingly—just as we ask participants to do.

I use codings that reinforce the theory, including: "5" next to those items that would not have been on your list five years ago; "M" or "F" next to those items that would be (or would have been) on your mother's or father's lists (or "G" for guardian); a day or date next to the last time you did that item; and so on. I give a second set of codings for the "old-timers" group.

"I Learned" Statements

I post a list of "I Learned" Statements (#15) just as participants are finishing their last coding. I ask them to write down one or, if there is time, two sentences that represent learnings derived from their lists of twenty things. Then I ask for volunteers to read one of their sentences aloud. I take quite a few, so people hear a large variety.

Then I talk a bit about the pedagogy of what we have done—how "I Learned" Statements can be used after many different activities; how Twenty Things You Love To Do is only one of many inventories; how they can be adjusted for different age levels, such as Ten Things You Love To Do, for older elementary students; Twenty Things That Use Electricity (during an energy crisis); and so on.

Here-and-Now Wheel

If I have time, I will do a Here-and-Now Wheel before lunch. This is the one in which participants close their eyes, identify four feelings they are experiencing, write down the four feeling words in four quarters of a wheel (or sections of a pie or quadrants of a circle), and expand one of the words into a longer phrase or sentence. Then I call on about five volunteers to read their Here-and-Now Wheels aloud, to get a sense of where the group is as we break for lunch.

We have accomplished several things this first morning. My list of strategies posted up front contains the following: 1—Comfort and Caring, 2—Value Name Tags, 3—Milling, 4—Sharing Trios, 5—Picker-Pickee, 6—Unfinished Business, 7—Twenty Things, 8—"I Learned" Statements, 9—Inventories, 10—Here-and-Now Wheel. By this time, participants have interacted, shared some important thoughts and feelings and experiences, and met and listened to a variety of people. They also have spoken "off the top of their heads," written and reflected, and heard the theory behind value clarification. We began by creating a sense of community through Comfort and Caring and Milling. We ended with the whole group together, sharing "I Learned" Statements and Here-and-Now Wheels. They have experienced much of the variety of value clarification and expect that more will come. It has been safe for them throughout. They are ready and eager to grow and learn (Here-and-Now Wheels often reflect this). If, indeed, I accomplish all this on the first morning, I am very pleased.

Lunch

No special hints about this, except that I might take some time before the Here-and-Now Wheel to see if anyone needs a ride, etc.

FIRST AFTERNOON
Singing

Because I play the guitar and sing, and so do some of my colleagues with whom I often work, I frequently have some music after lunch.

Three songs is my limit and I like them to be mostly sing-alongs, which people know or can easily follow. Of course, this is strictly a personal preference, and I would not advocate a singing period for those who feel uncomfortable trying it.

Question Period

This is a good time for a few questions or comments from the group. Most people's attention is fairly high. Fifteen minutes is enough time. The problem with the question-and-answer mode is that many of the questions interest only a few of the participants. I try to encourage people to see me during breaks and before and after sessions with their questions, but a couple of question periods during the workshop is fine, so long as they do not go on too long.

In answering questions, one thing I have learned from Merrill Harmin is to be brief. There was the time someone asked him, "Would you say that. . . ?" and went on with a very long and theoretical question. His answer was "Probably." I tend to err in the direction of being too long-winded in my responses: If someone asks me, "How do you handle discipline problems?" I assume the questioner has thought about this issue from every angle and wants to hear me speak of it from every angle. So if I happen to have eight pieces of wisdom on the subject, I feel compelled to share them all. This is almost always a mistake. The group will profit much more from a two-minute answer, leaving eight minutes to become involved in a new strategy, than they will from a ten-minute statement.

Voting (#3), Ranking (#4), and Continuum (#8)

I ask people to get into groups of six and begin a sequence of activities involving these three "bread and butter" strategies, so called because they are staples in the value clarifier's diet, able to be used over and over again on different occasions.

Because many participants may be familiar with these strategies, if I have a team-teacher, this is a good time to offer an alternative session, with some "advanced" strategies for those already familiar with Voting, Ranking, and the Continuum.

I explain how voting works, give participants a chance to try out the signals (i.e., "What do you do if I ask about something you really like a lot?"), and then ask them to vote on ten questions, which I have prepared beforehand. (The voting takes place in the groups of six.) I encourage them to look around their sextet and see the diversity. Once most of them have voted on a question, I vote also. Finally, I take a couple of minutes to talk about how the voting strategy can be used in classes and groups.

Now I ask them to divide their group of six in half to form two groups of three, and I give them two rank orders, writing down the items in front of the room. I ask each person to individually rank both rank orders. Then, reminding people of their right to pass, I ask them each to take a turn of one or two minutes to select one of the rank orders and share their thinking on it with the other two members of their trio. When they are done, I tell them how I ranked one of the rank orders and share my thinking. Again, I take a few minutes to explain how the rank order can be used in various settings.

At this point, the original sextets are re-formed. I post a continuum up front, and ask members, in their sextets, to have someone draw a similar continuum; then all six persons place themselves on the continuum and explain their position and I place myself on the continuum up front. This is a good time to take a few minutes to call attention to my role—how I, as a value-clarification teacher, am willing to be involved in the process myself, and how I try to share but not impose my values, how I wish to be a model and not a moralizer.

Now I ask participants to divide into threes again. I ask them to select one of the areas of confusion and conflict in values (these have been posted since the morning) and, working together as a group, come up with five voting questions, two rank orders (or one, if I am short on time), and one continuum on that topic. (I ask them to make up questions that particularly interest them—because they will also have an opportunity to ask another trio the questions they create.) I let them know I will check back with them in fifteen minutes to see how they are doing and ask them to call me over if they need any help. I make myself available for the next fifteen minutes. Then I check to see how the groups are doing and give up to five extra minutes to complete the task.

Now I explain in precise detail what comes next. They are to divide their "production" among the three members of their trio—one person taking the voting questions, another taking the rank orders, another taking the continuum—and then regroup into their original sextet. The person in charge of voting from the first trio will then read the five voting questions his or her trio made up, and all six people will vote, the "leader" behaving just as he or she would with students, e.g., accepting, voting last, etc. Then the voting person from the second trio will read the voting questions from his or her trio, and again, all six will vote. Then, the "rank order" person from the first trio will present the rank orders his or her trio created, and all six will give their ranking. And so on through the second set of rank orders and both continuums. I emphasize that members should not discuss their responses because they could get into an argument over the first voting question and no others will get a chance to ask questions before the time runs out. Let me emphasize that it is a good idea to explain this whole procedure in detail before participants begin; it is a somewhat complex procedure, and if they do not hear and understand the directions, it is easy to get confused. I allow about fifteen to twenty minutes for this whole procedure and suggest they move into their break when they are finished.

Break

After the break, I ask for some "I Learned" Statements or questions based on the participants' experience in the practice session. I think a practice session like this is very important. It helps them build confidence in their ability to actually utilize the strategies; it reinforces their belief in their ability to create their own questions; and it makes it more likely that they will use the strategies back home.

Public Interview (#12)

I explain how a Public Interview works and ask for volunteers. I select a volunteer and conduct a ten-minute Public Interview. As usual, I explain the purpose of this strategy by referring to the valuing processes that are exercised by it.

Group Interview (#14)

I or my team-teacher volunteers to receive a Group Interview. I will answer honestly, but just as any group member can do in an interview, I will pass or tell only part of my story whenever that seems appropriate. If I have some values or beliefs or behaviors that are considerably different from the group I am working with, I walk a fine line. I want to expose them to some alternatives, which they are likely to attend to because I have won their respect during the course of the day. On the other hand, if the alternatives from my life are so very different from their own values that they might be shocked or that their trust in me could fall considerably, this attitude could transfer itself to value clarification and I might defeat my own purposes for doing the workshop in the first place. So in situations like this, my guideline is to be as honest as I can, up to the point where I start to destroy the relationship I have been building. Then I pass, or at least I do not go into detail. It becomes a matter of priorities for me. My main goal is to present value clarification as an attractive alternative that they will understand and want to use in their own settings. Sharing my own views on politics or religion or whatever is much less important to me, and I will not allow the latter to jeopardize the former.

Group Interview Practice

I ask people to get into groups of four to six, depending on how much time is available. I make sure there is a watch in each group, unless a clock is visible to all. At any rate, each group should have its own timekeeper. I explain that people will now get a chance to practice what they just saw demonstrated, that is, giving and receiving a Group Interview. Each person gets six minutes to receive a Group Interview from his or her group. I emphasize several guidelines:

1. Do not "psychoanalyze" the person or try to solve his or her problems. The goals of this exercise are to get to know the person better and to ask some good, thought-provoking, value-clarifying questions (ones that require the use of valuing processes to answer).

2. Strike a balance between questions of information and clarifying questions, and between questions about professions and about other topics.

3. Do not allow more than two questions in a row from any one person. (This rule prevents the questioning from turning into a one-on-one public interview.)

I Wonder Statements

If there is enough time left, I like to bring the whole group together and close with I Wonder Statements. This is a nice way to end the day. It re-creates the sense of community, bridges the gap to the back-home world ("I wonder what my family would think if I asked them some rank orders tonight"), and points the group's attention toward the next day ("I wonder what tomorrow will be like").

SECOND MORNING

In a Saturday-Sunday workshop, I can be quite certain that some people will come in late on Sunday morning. Here I have a choice. I can start late, an alternative I spoke of earlier that has few advantages and many disadvantages; or I can begin on time, with an activity that latecomers will be able to get involved in without distracting the people who have been involved from the beginning. The last alternative is invariably my decision.

Either-Or (#5)

Given the above consideration, I open with the Either-Or Forced Choice strategy. I ask the group to stand and come to the center of the room, and I post the two choices on opposite walls. They go to the side of their choice and find someone to talk to. Then they come back to the center. By now a few stragglers have come in, and I ask them to join the group in the center of the room. "Are you more like a *forest* or a *street*?" Again they divide, pair, and discuss. Back to the center. A few more latecomers join the group. A third choice. And so on. We have succeeded in starting promptly at 9:00 A.M., taken care of the latecomer problem, and gotten everyone actively involved in a light, new strategy—a good beginning for the second day.

Value Journal (#17)

I ask people to take their seats, and I bring both lists of Either-Or choices up front. If, for instance, I am giving them five choices, I ask them to write in their notebook, or "Value Journal," the five words or phrases they moved toward during the Either-Or exercise. Then I ask them to take five minutes of time alone to "write a paragraph or two about the kind of person who would make those five choices you have in front of you." I do not say much more in the way of directions, since I want them to exercise some creativity in this task. I write a paragraph, too. I whisper a one-minute-more time signal. When the time is up, I call on three or four volunteers to read their paragraphs. If I feel like it, I read my own. It is usually very interesting to see how people move from the light Either-Or exercise to the writing of some very reflective personal explorations. It certainly reinforces the theory that even the fun-filled value-clarification strategies have the potential for serious value exploration.

Then I talk a little about the Value Journal, one of the most important value-clarification strategies, but one that is not usually mentioned in value-clarification workshops. I explain its purpose and the different ways it might be used. I believe that if the Value Journal were used more widely, fewer people would think of value clarification as a "superficial" approach. The Value Journal helps build reflection, integration, and cumulative impact into a series of value-clarification experiences.

Subject Matter

By this time I can be fairly certain that the subject-matter teachers in the group, including drug, sex, and religious educators, have been thinking, "Well, all this is very nice, but how does it relate to the content I teach as part of my work?" Not everyone in the workshop has this concern, so if I have a team-teacher, this is a good time to give participants a choice of sessions. The alternative could be a different strategy. For the subject-matter group, I present the three-levels conception of subject matter, give some examples, entertain some questions, and hand out a list of value-clarification materials they can order that are related to English, history, math, science, and so forth.

Break

During the break, I set up about eight chairs in front of the room for a demonstration group.

Panel

I explain that I would like to use a panel of volunteers to demonstrate quickly about five or six strategies that would take much longer to do with the entire group. I ask for volunteers to come up and fill in the seats. Then, going up and down the line, I do such strategies as the Proud Whip (#11), Magic Box (#34), "I Urge" Telegrams (#44), Value Whip (#10), Pages from an Autobiography (#36), and, if I have not done it before, the "I Wonder" Statements (#16). I participate on occasion myself. After each one, I say a little about how it can be used or adapted in classrooms or other settings.

Thought-Feel Sheets (Part I)

Before leaving for lunch, I ask everyone to write a "Thought-Feel Sheet" (Merrill Harmin's synthesis of a Thought Sheet and a Here-and-Now Wheel). They write some thoughts they are thinking on one side and some feelings they are feeling on the other side. No names. I tell them to write "Please do not read to group" if they prefer not to have their sheets read aloud.

Lunch

SECOND AFTERNOON

Thought-Feel Sheets (Part II)

I read twenty or thirty to the workshop, about half thoughts, half feelings. There is no discussion. I explain how these can be used with classes or groups. I might mention Value Cards (see *Values and Teaching*, 1966) in this context.

Focus Game (#18)

I think this is an essential value-clarification strategy. If students can learn to focus, any strategy, either in a small or large group, automatically becomes much more effective. In some classes, it becomes possible, for the first time, to use small groups.

I ask them to form trios, I explain the three focus rules, and I describe how the exercise will work. Each person will get five minutes as focus person to express his or her thoughts and feelings on the subject to be designated. The other two follow the focus rules. Then the second person will talk on the same subject, while the first and third follow the focus rules. Finally the third person will be the focus.

Then I use the Devil's Advocate Strategy (see *Values and Teaching*, 1966) to provide a good topic for discussion. I might talk on the fortunate death of marriage as an institution, or give an outrageous proposal for solving world economic problems, or argue that schools should be eliminated altogether, or whatever. When I finish, the first focus person begins, and the second and third follow the focus rules.

After five minutes, I interrupt and have people draw three continuums, from 0 to 10. Each continuum corresponds to a focus rule. I ask the focus person to indicate how well he or she felt *focused on*, *accepted*, and *drawn out*, by putting a check on each line, 0 being the lowest score, 10 the highest. I ask the two "helpers" to rate themselves, individually, on how well they thought they focused, accepted, and drew out the focus person. I ask them to cover their responses and begin the second round.

After the second round, I ask them to repeat the same rating system but this time to share their perceptions and feelings with one another. I explain just a little about feedback, especially how it is most helpful when it is most specific; for example, "You had a look on your face something like this, which made me think you were disapproving of what I was saying, so I felt kind of frightened of you and not accepted," or "That one question you asked me made it very easy for me to talk," etc. I allow the feedback to go on for about five minutes. On the running list of strategies, I have written Devil's Advocate, Self-Evaluation, and Group Feedback to remind people that this sequence is teaching not only the Focus Game, but also three other reproducible strategies.

Then comes the third round and, if there is time, another self-evaluation and group feedback. I talk a little about using the Focus Game.

Back-Home Focus

This is not so much a strategy as an opportunity for participants to apply their learnings to their back-home situation. I help people to get into groups of similar interest—English teachers, elementary teachers, administrators, drug-abuse educators, people who came as a team, people wanting to focus on their family, and so on. I aim for groups of two to five, since larger ones tend to be less productive in this activity. People without a group have a choice of working individually, sitting in another group, or doing something else. Their task is to relate what they have learned at the workshop to their back-home setting in order to increase the likelihood that they will accomplish what they want to back home.

I try to allow a half hour to an hour of work time, depending on how fast or slow the clock seems to be moving that afternoon. They can use the time as they wish, but I make a few suggestions, based on my past experience with work groups of this type. I very briefly describe Brainstorming (#25) and suggest they might take part or all of their time to brainstorm ways to apply what they learned to their work—a Rank Order they can think of, a good third-level question, an inventory, a use of the Focus Game, a Proud Whip, etc. If they can think of thirty ideas, maybe five to ten will have possibilities for each individual in the group. I also suggest that they can each have five or ten minutes of focus time to talk about their back-home situation and what they plan to do. Sometimes I also suggest Force-Field Analysis (#22) as a way of analyzing their back-home situation.

During the participants' work time, I float around from group to group and to the individuals without a group, helping as I can. I avoid taking over the groups by encouraging them to work alone for a while and then to call me over for any specific questions they may have.

I ask the groups and individuals to reconvene and I share some of my own thoughts or experiences about "re-entry" and back-home applications. Sometimes this is done in the form of skits, exaggerating what some people do when they enthusiastically return home. For example: "What was the workshop like?" "Oh, (glassy-eyed) you wouldn't understand; you would have to have been there."

Loose Ends

This is the time for some final questions and answers and any announcements I or participants have to make. It is the last chance to ask for a ride home, for me to get a ride to the airport, and for me to do any resource sharing I want to do about other workshops, publications, etc. I do all this now in order not to take away from the impact of the last strategy.

IALAC

I tell Sidney Simon's IALAC story (Argus, 1973) in a way that seems comfortable to me. I vary the main character and the incidents that happen to him or her, as I wish. I do wear an IALAC sign and rip or add pieces as needed. I briefly talk about some of the ways IALAC can be used with students and other groups. I say good-bye and thanks to the group in whatever way seems right to me then. Perhaps I ask them to join me in one last song.

SUMMARY

In this two-day workshop, I shared with the group the most important pieces of the value-clarification theory and a good portion of the most useful value-clarification strategies I know. I tried to use the strategies that participants could use again and again, rather than the ones they would use only once. Not only were they involved and active most of the time, they also had a chance to practice building skills—creating and using voting, ranking, and continua; interviewing; and focusing. And I tried to help in the transition from the workshop to their back-home realities.

The biggest drawback of this design, I think, is that it may try to do too much in two days. I have to continually keep things moving along if I am going to "cover the curriculum." That is a strain on me and a pressure on the participants. And it does not model the pace I would recommend that they use with students. However, the fact that I have continued to use this design, or ones like it, indicates my belief that it works in spite of this drawback. For me, it has proved to be a very satisfactory design for a two-day value-clarification workshop.

REFERENCES

Raths, L. E., Harmin, M., & Simon, S. B. *Values and teaching.* Columbus, Ohio: Charles E. Merrill, 1966.

Simon, S. B., Howe, L., & Kirschenbaum, H. *Values clarification: A handbook of practical strategies for teachers and students.* New York, Hart: 1972.

Chapter 7

DESIGNS FOR SHORTER AND LONGER WORKSHOPS

LONGER WORKSHOPS AND COURSES

In workshops or courses longer than two days, I use the two-day design as my basic model, but I make the following alterations:

1. I try to go a bit more slowly. This seems obvious; with more time, there is not quite the need to move along so rapidly. Ironically, I find I do not go much more slowly. Even if I had two weeks, I would probably still feel there is "so much" I want to do.

2. I do more strategies, of course. The Clarifying Response and Value Sheet (both from *Values and Teaching*), the Free Choice Game (#52), and Self-Contracts (#59), are among my priorities for new strategies to insert in the design. I also do some of the more game-like ones, such as Alligator River (#50), Coat of Arms (#47), Forced-Choice Ladder (#6), and so on. However, I prefer to use strategies that teach the participants basic value-clarification skills, which they can use over and over again when they leave. In other words, if I have to make a choice between strategies that require a bit more "work" but teach basic skills and ones that are more fun but can be repeated only once or twice, I choose the former.

3. I include more theory. I think it is important to keep reinforcing the value theory, to add pieces to it, and to approach it from different angles. The theory has many facets and ramifications for education and human development. It is a mistake, I think, to assume that one rendition of the basic theory is enough. A longer workshop provides the opportunity to include these additions. Some of the pieces I typically add are the following:

- the relationship between value needs and emotional needs (from *Values and Teaching*, and Raths & Burrell, 1963);

- Rogers' conception of how feelings get separated from values (Rogers, 1964), and my conception of how we can re-integrate them;
- the difference between *im*posing, *de*posing, and *ex*posing values;
- how value clarification proceeds by creating a climate of acceptance, eliciting information, accepting that information, clarifying it, accepting it, eliciting more information and clarifying it more, accepting it, and so on;
- some research on attitude change that seems relevant;
- theory and research from psychotherapy, moral development, creativity, learning theory, group dynamics, or whatever theory and research seems appropriate at the time;
- whatever theory emerges during question-and-answer period.

4. I add more practice. I provide experiences in trying out clarifying responses, conducting clarifying interviews, making up value sheets, and asking third-level (value-level, "you") questions. For reasons stated in the preceding chapter on designing two-day workshops, I think practice is very important.
tice is very important.

5. I allow more time for participants who have used value clarification to share some of the things they have done.

6. Longer workshops tend to promote more of a social life. Coffee and donut committees provide refreshments for breaks, participants chipping in a dime or a quarter each day to pay for the goodies. A party committee may organize a picnic or party, local people may invite out-of-towners home for dinner, and so on. When it is appropriate, I encourage and even facilitate this socializing. As mentioned earlier, one of my four objectives is that people will leave the workshop with a positive attitude toward value clarification—and good times help this attitude.

7. In longer workshops for a given system and in on-going training programs, I use more team-building strategies, Force-Field Analysis (#22), and action-planning strategies.

A ONE-DAY WORKSHOP: TWO DESIGNS

Design I

For a one-day workshop, I frequently use the same design as the one described for the first day of the two-day workshop. The format would look like the following:

Morning	Afternoon
Introduction	Voting
Value Name Tags*	Ranking
Milling	Continuum
Sharing Trios	Practice
Break	Break
Theory	Public Interview
Twenty Things	Group Interview
"I Learned" Statements	Practice
Here-and-Now Wheel	I Wonder Statements

For a detailed description of how and why these strategies are used and how they fit together, refer to the description of the two-day design in Chapter 6. As indicated earlier, this design provides a group with a good introduction to value clarification—consisting of theory, experience, and practice.

Design II

I frequently use this design when working with a school or school system. If it is a small group, the workshop may take place in a classroom. More often, it is a larger group, and we work in the school cafeteria or auditorium. I have used this design with groups ranging from thirty to several hundred members. For purposes of visualizing the group context, imagine me on a stage or platform with a chalkboard and about eight or ten empty chairs behind me. (I like to work with poster paper taped to the board and heavy black markers, but chalk works too, if I write heavily enough and the room is not too large.)

INTRODUCTION

To begin, I spend fifteen or twenty minutes talking about the confusion and conflict in values that most young people experience today and about the various ways of helping people with these value problems. This brief lecture essentially consists of the first two pieces of the value-clarification theory, as discussed in Chapter 2. I explain that value clarification teaches a valuing process, which the other approaches do not; however, I add that before explaining that process in

---

*Note that in the remainder of the text, strategy numbers as they appear in the *Values Clarification Handbook* will be eliminated except when a strategy is introduced for the first time.

greater detail, I will demonstrate some practical strategies designed to teach students how the process works.

What I try to do here is to give the demonstration that follows a context and some credibility. I also try not to bore the participants this early in the morning. Their energy is usually low, their expectations—based on previous in-service days—are probably low, and I want to proceed with something interesting and not delay it with a long speech.

DEMONSTRATION

Before I arrive, I arrange with the principal or assistant superintendent, or whomever, to select a panel of students to serve as a demonstration group. With a K–12 audience, I ask for a cross section of fourth-through twelfth-graders. With high school teachers, I ask for high school students, and the same with the junior high level. With elementary teachers, I request fourth- through sixth-graders. (I find that below fourth grade, students may be too shy to speak in front of an audience of teachers; I do not like to take the chance, although sometimes I do it.) If I am working with teachers of former school drop-outs, I ask for a panel of former drop-outs, and so on. I make it clear that I am not looking for their "best" students, but for a cross section of ability levels, ethnic groups, or whatever groups exist in that school and community.

The students then come out on the stage. I have arranged for them to have large name tags, which can be easily read, so that I can call them by their names. I may or may not have met them backstage before this moment. In any case, I review their names aloud to help me learn them and I explain to them, with the audience listening, what we are going to do. Here I emphasize that *there are no right answers* and that *they always have the right to pass*—in this way they need never worry that they are going to give the wrong answer or that they will be embarrassed by being caught without something to say. At any time, they can say, "I pass," and we will go right on to the next person. Clearly, I am trying to help them relax and keep them informed about what is going to happen. The more I do this type of demonstration, the more confident and relaxed I feel, which in turn is communicated to the students.

Sometimes I ask a couple of teachers to volunteer to join the panel to show that value clarification is really a life-long process. That is usually fun; the audience identifies with them very strongly, so there is a lot of laughter as the audience discharges its own embarrassment at the mere thought of sitting up there like that. It is also funny for the members of the audience to see their colleagues in that incongruous setting. It works well, as long as I am careful to let the students respond first most of the time, so the teachers do not dominate and set the tone.

I explain to the audience that the five activities I am about to demonstrate are "the tip of the iceberg." I suggest that each one could be followed by extended discussion or other activities that build upon these. I want to avoid having people think that value clarification is simply a list of voting questions or a five-minute rank order. Unfortunately, that is probably how many people get the impression that value clarification is something "superficial." I let them know that these are only "starters," that there are several hundred strategies designed to teach the valuing process (which I will describe a bit later).

I generally do five of the "bread and butter" strategies with the panel: Value Voting (ten questions), Rank Orders (two), Continuum (one), Proud Whip (one), and a Public Interview. I do not feel the need to have every panel member respond to every strategy. I may stop in the middle of the row and continue with the next person on the next strategy.

I use these five strategies because the teachers watching can use them with relative ease in their own classrooms and can use them many times by creating their own, new examples. The strategies can also be done fairly quickly. I take from forty minutes to an hour with the demonstration, depending on time considerations. After each strategy, I take a couple of minutes to give some examples of how it can be used in the classroom or to say a little on what the strategy does. For example, after the Proud Whip, I might take a few moments to point out what little time we normally take to help students be aware of what makes them proud; instead, we give them plenty of opportunities to learn about what they do wrong, what they could do better, and so on. and so on.

I participate myself, voting just after most of the students have committed themselves. I indicate my rank orders, and place myself on the continuum after they have, and tell something I am proud of, and perhaps give the student I interviewed a chance to ask me two or three of the questions I asked him or her. At some point I call attention to my role—how I am quite willing to share and model my values, but not in an imposing or moralizing way.

I thank the students as they leave, and perhaps ask the audience to give them a round of applause.

BREAK

THEORY

Here I explain the valuing process. If the group is small, I might take a few questions, but I do not want this to run longer than twenty minutes. Lately, I have begun handing out a paper with the valuing process outlined on one side and further materials on value clarification on the other side. This facilitates the lecture.

TWENTY THINGS

As a way of illustrating the theory, I involve the whole group in Twenty Things You Love To Do, with the codings and variation I described in the two-day design (Chapter 6).

"I LEARNED" STATEMENTS

I invite "I Learned" Statements from the group. Even if there are hundreds of people in the audience, and even if I have to repeat each volunteer's "I Learned" Statements for others to hear, it still works. There is something about the spontaneity of the demonstration, the inventory of Twenty Things, and the "I Learned" Statements that enables even a resistant audience to appreciate to some degree what is happening.

LUNCH

PRACTICE SESSION

I explain that the afternoon will be devoted to involving the participants in some more strategies and also to dealing with the question of how value clarification relates to the teaching of traditional school subject areas. I find it important to say this, so that those subject-matter-oriented teachers, who may be wondering where the relevance is in all this to their needs, can hold out a little longer, confident that their concerns will be dealt with.

Then I ask participants to form groups of threes *with two others they do not know very well*, and I lead a practice session exactly like the one in the two-day workshop (Chapter 6). I emphasize that they are to choose topics they are interested in themselves and create questions, rank orders, and continua that other adults could respond to. I share the principle that if they learn the process of creating these types of value questions, they can then apply it to any age group and subject area they are familiar with. If I am short on time, I may cut back on the number of items they are to create. Then they join another trio, etc. I allow forty to fifty minutes for the entire sequence.

SUBJECT-MATTER THEORY

If the group is small enough, I may ask for "I Learned" Statements or questions based on the practice session. Then I briefly state the three-levels theory, with examples, and call participants' attention to further resources, as I did in the two-day workshop.

BREAK (if one is scheduled)

ALLIGATOR RIVER

At this time of the afternoon, after the practice session and more theory, people are ready for a lighter strategy. I like Alligator River (#50), which I tell my own way and which I follow up with my own sequence of clarifying steps; for example, "Spend one minute telling your quartet how, in terms of your actual behavior, you are *not like* the top character on your list." This is an enjoyable way to end the day. As has been true throughout the workshop, even resistant audience members have been able to get involved without much trouble.

I summarize the day, thank the group, and make announcements.

There are an infinite number of one-day workshop designs I might have described, but these designs are two of my favorites and have given me much valuable service over the years and brought many teachers and others to value clarification.

SHORTER WORKSHOPS AND PRESENTATIONS

This section offers two designs for a two-and-one-half- to three-hour session and two designs for a one- to one-and-one-half-hour presentation. Three hours is equivalent to a full morning, afternoon, or evening session—the type of presentation I am often asked to do for a school faculty or parent group.

Two-and-One-Half- to Three-Hour Workshops: Design I

The morning session of the second one-day design, previously described in greater detail, makes an excellent, short presentation-workshop. It includes: a brief theoretical introduction, a panel to demonstrate five value-clarification strategies, a break, a brief lecture on the valuing process, Twenty Things, and "I Learned" Statements. There may be time for some questions and answers, too. In that brief period, the participants hear some major parts of the theory and see or experience seven strategies, all of which they can take back to their classrooms, homes, or work settings.

If it is a school setting, I ask for a student panel, as described earlier in this chapter. In a nonschool setting, I usually ask for volunteers from the audience to fill the chairs up front. I do not do this beforehand; volunteers are solicited when I am ready for them. This spontaneous process generates a good deal of excitement, since the audience members realize they could very well be up there themselves, and they know there is nothing staged about this demonstration.

If it is a school setting, I also make certain that I spend at least five minutes on the subject-matter applications of value clarification. I mention that every subject area in the curriculum can be taught on three levels—facts, concepts, and values—and that there is a series of articles on how to teach English, history, math, science, etc., with a focus on values. I then make available a materials list that includes these articles. This helps satisfy the teachers' concern that value clarification be related to their own subject areas.

Two-and-One-Half- to Three-Hour Workshops: Design II

With an entire faculty (that is, a group that *had to* come to this inservice session or workshop), I almost always use the preceding design. It enables them to participate vicariously at first and get personally involved a little later. But with volunteer groups and other types of groups, I sometimes use the following design. It foregoes the panel in favor of having everyone personally involved throughout the session.

VOTING

I begin with some informational voting questions and some questions that help people chuckle a bit and relax. "How many of you are pretty tired right now?" "How many of you wish you were somewhere else right now?" "How many of you have ever been to a workshop or seen a demonstration of value clarification?" And so on. (This may take about five minutes.)

THEORY

I introduce the areas of confusion and conflict and the ways of helping people with values. I do not describe the valuing process yet. (Fifteen minutes.)

NAME-TAG OR OTHER GET-TO-KNOW-YOU STRATEGIES

I have participants do a Value Name Tag, or I use or invent some other type of ice-breaker strategy. For example, I might ask them five name-tag-type questions, such as "Where is a place you'd love to spend a year?" "What are two things you do well?" and so on. Instead of having them write the answers on their name tags, I have them write the questions and answers on a piece of paper.

MILLING

With the regular name tag they will mill around, as usual, reading each others' name tags. Using the variation mentioned above, participants mill around with the sheet of paper, and then I ask them to pair off. They get to ask their partners one of the five questions. If the partner does not want to answer that question, he or she can answer another one of the five. The partner then asks a question. Pairs switch partners and repeat the procedure. And again, a third time. (The name tag and milling sequence takes about fifteen minutes. The variation would be five to ten minutes longer.) At the conclusion of the milling procedure, I ask participants to form trios with people they do not know, if possible.

RANK ORDERS

I give them two Rank Orders and ask each person to take two minutes to give his or her rankings on both, and his or her reasoning on one. I explain the right to pass. After everyone has finished, I talk a little about the Rank-Order strategy (Fifteen minutes). Then I ask each trio to combine with another trio, forming a sextet.

VALUE VOTING

I ask some more voting questions, this time with a stronger value focus. I have people look around their group to see how people are voting. I talk a bit about the Voting strategy. (Ten minutes.)

CONTINUUM

I draw a continuum on the board and ask participants to select someone in their sextet to draw one like it. Then all members of each group are asked to place their names somewhere along the continuum and explain their positions. I talk a bit about the Continuum strategy. (Fifteen minutes.)

PROUD WHIP

I present the Proud Whip, introduce a topic, and have each person in the sextets take a turn. As in the other strategies, I participate, too, at the end. (Ten minutes.)

What I have done so far, in effect, is to make each sextet a panel in itself, so that everyone gets to participate. I lose the chance to model the more direct interaction between facilitator and participant that happens in the demonstration panel, but I do model a different teacher behavior—how to use small groups.

BREAK

THEORY

I describe the valuing process and the four ways that value clarification teaches it. (Twenty minutes.)

TWENTY THINGS (Twenty minutes.)

"I LEARNED" STATEMENTS (Ten minutes.)

The rest of the morning is the same as in the previous design.

One- to One-and-One-Half-Hour Presentations: Design I

This design is intended to present the theory and demonstrate five strategies in a very brief period. I have used it with audiences of up to fifteen hundred people.

THEORY

If I have only an hour, I begin with a fifteen- to twenty-minute lecture on value-clarification theory. If I have an hour and one-half, I take twenty to twenty-five minutes.

PANEL

As described earlier, I use a panel of students or audience volunteers to demonstrate the Voting, Ranking, Continuum, Proud Whip, and Public Interview strategies. I need to move quickly. If I am short on time, I delete one of the later strategies. In the hour presentation, if I have lectured for fifteen minutes, I take forty minutes for the demonstration. In the one-and-one-half-hour presentation, if I have lectured for twenty minutes, I take an hour for the demonstration.

CLOSING

I have five or ten minutes left. I say whatever I need to about the demonstration and any last points I want to make. If I have ten minutes and not much to say, I take two or three questions from the audience and make a brief concluding statement, leaving behind a list of materials and workshops for those interested.

One- to One-And-One-Half-Hour Presentations: Design II

This design is used with smaller groups—about ten to forty participants. Again, it sacrifices the panel for more audience involvement.

I have all participants put their chairs in a circle or horseshoe arrangement, but in such a way that they can see the chalkboard or wherever my charts are posted.

THEORY

I present the theory as in the previous design.

VALUES VOTING

I ask the whole group some voting questions and talk about the strategy.

RANKING

I give a rank order and, starting at some point in the circle, ask the first six people to respond. I give my ranking. I post another rank order and ask the next six people to do the ranking. I give mine. In demonstrations, I sometimes ask if two or three people would care to give their reasoning or what they thought about when they were processing the rank order. Then I say a bit about the strategy.

CONTINUUM

I post a continuum and ask the next six people or so to place themselves on the line and explain their positions. I identify and explain my position and discuss the strategy.

PROUD WHIP

I continue this model by using the Proud Whip strategy.

PUBLIC INTERVIEW

I explain the strategy, ask for a volunteer, and conduct a Public Interview. Perhaps I ask for a volunteer who has not yet had a chance to participate.

CONCLUSION

If I have time, I take a few questions; if not, I simply conclude, taking a few minutes to summarize and to mention further resources.

This design works very well because the participants feel more like a group than an audience. I also enjoy greater eye contact and interaction with them.

DESIGN FOR COUNSELOR-ORIENTED GROUPS

Increasingly, counselors, therapists, mental-health workers, social workers, nurse-counselors, pastor-counselors, and other counseling-

oriented individuals are showing a greater interest in value clarification and are attending more and more value-clarification workshops.
Personnel and guidance associations and various mental health and
crisis centers have also been increasing their requests for value-
clarification consultants to come to their areas and work with their
personnel. As a result, I have found it necessary to somewhat alter my
workshop emphasis for this professional audience.

When invited to give a workshop for any of these professional
groups, I try to discover, as soon as possible, the type of counseling
work the participants are involved in. Primarily, I am interested in
knowing whether their orientation is toward group or one-to-one counseling. If I find that a large number of people work exclusively with
individual clients, then I avoid most of the group-oriented value-
clarification strategies in favor of the strategies that lend themselves
to one-to-one relationships. Also, I almost always give greater emphasis to the clarifying response. Initially value clarification was primarily used as a counseling model; only later did it move toward the group
strategies. Thus, the clarifying response is the most basic tool of value
clarification, and in this type of situation I highlight this clarifying
response early in the theory presentation, using the continuum of helping responses (see Chapter 2). I find this continuum particularly useful
for counseling groups because many of them are very familiar with the
Rogerian client-centered mode of helping. If they are staunch client-
centered advocates, it is important to acknowledge their school of
thought and show how the clarifying response is different but complementary. If they are opposed to client-centered thinking, then it is
important to show how the clarifying response is qualitatively different from the purely empathic response (though similar in ultimate
goal).

What follows is a typical design I might use for teaching the clarifying response.

1. I post or pass out a list of Incomplete Sentences (#37) and ask
each person to complete five or six of them. I ask for several volunteers
to complete one of their sentences aloud. After a person completes a
sentence, I ask him or her two or three clarifying questions about what
he or she said. The person then responds to my questions. I do not
extend it into a Public Interview—just two or three questions. Then I
call on another person, and so on.

2. After doing this with about four people, I stop and explain what
I was trying to do. I explain the clarifying response in greater detail
than I have before, relating it to the valuing process. I hand out a

sheet, from *Values and Teaching*, with the list of thirty typical clarifying responses. I give a talk, based on my experience, about how the clarifying response should be a spontaneous, relevant response to what a person says, not a rehearsed, read-it-off-the-list-of-thirty type of response, which leaves the person wondering what you are trying to "do to" him. The response should come out of your interest in the other person as well as from a desire to assist in his or her value clarification. If it does not, the response will sound phony and the person will mistrust your question.

3. I ask for some more volunteers to complete a sentence aloud; this time, however, I ask volunteers from the group to ask the clarifying questions. I try to be supportive, keep it moving, and keep evaluation to a minimum. If it seems appropriate, I might ask the interviewee, "How did that question make you feel?" I want to avoid "grading" the responses. Often a question that would make one person very defensive is very clarifying for another person.

4. I ask them to continue this procedure in groups of threes. One person completes a sentence; the other two make one or two clarifying responses. Then the second person completes a sentence, and the first and third persons ask a few questions. And so on, more than once around if there is time. Again, I offer encouragement, reminding the participants that this is being done out of context and thus it is not unlike practicing scales in order to learn to play a musical instrument.

5. Often this approach works very well. Sometimes, though, people resist it because it feels so unnatural at first. They cannot quite see how it can be helpful or how it would work in a more natural setting. So I frequently conduct a "Clarifying Interview" in front of the group and show how the clarifying response is used in a very real helping situation. Usually I interview my team-teacher; sometimes, a member of the group. The interviewee shares a choice he or she is facing that is posing a dilemma. I listen empathically and I ask clarifying questions, following the model suggested in the "Free Choice Game" (#52). Once people have seen the potency of the clarifying question or response, used in this typical conversational setting, they are much more ready to practice this form of questioning—much as one practices any new skill.

Once I have done some work with the clarifying question, it also becomes easier to teach other strategies, since the participants can now see how every strategy is a good clarifying question that has been structured and elaborated upon. A Rank Order or a Continuum, for example, can be a very clarifying question in a one-to-one interview— if it relates directly to the issues the person is grappling with.

In a one-day or longer workshop with counselors (and with others), I have mixed feelings about when to use this type of sequence for the clarifying response. Because it is so basic and provides such a good foundation for everything else in value clarification, I am tempted to do it near the beginning of the workshop. But it is very difficult to teach, and groups or individuals are sometimes resistant to it. So I also feel tempted to wait until later, once a sense of community has been built and the participants have had some sense of what nonmoralizing strategies (e.g., Voting questions, Rank Orders) are like. I have tried it both ways and still have not reached a definite conclusion.

REFERENCES

Raths, L. E., and Burrell, A. *Understanding the problem child*. Danville, N.J.: Economics Press, 1963.

Rogers, C. R. Toward a modern approach to values: The valuing process in the mature person. *Journal of Abnormal and Social Psychology*, 1964, 68, 2, 160–167. Chapter in Kirschenbaum, H. and Simon, S. B. (Eds.) *Readings in values clarification*. Minneapolis, Minn.: Winston Press, 1974.

Chapter 8

TRAINING A LARGE PUBLIC SCHOOL SYSTEM IN VALUE CLARIFICATION

Value clarification was introduced to the public school system in Akron, Ohio, as the result of the Assistant Superintendent of Curriculum and Instruction feeling the need to give teachers some new methods to use in teaching values to children. In 1969, the Akron City Schools and the Akron Council of Churches jointly sent eight people to a value-clarification workshop that Sidney Simon and I conducted in East Rochester, New York. When they returned, these eight teachers served as staff members for a workshop, which Simon and I led, that was attended by sixty-two teachers, approximately one from every school in Akron. For five days, from 9:00 A.M. to 3:30 P.M., the teachers were introduced to value-clarification methods. They returned to their classrooms in September highly motivated to use the strategies in their instructional program for the coming year.

THE FIRST YEAR

Ongoing activities the first year included an in-service meeting, a demonstration of value-clarification techniques Simon and I gave for over one thousand teachers, which represented the majority of the entire professional staff. At this time, teachers who wanted further training submitted forms indicating their interest. In late spring of 1970, several evening in-service meetings in value clarification were held, using teachers from the previous summer workshop as resource people. These meetings were a prerequisite to being considered for the

This chapter is adapted from the article "Training a Large Public School System in Values Clarification" by Diane Greene, Pat Stewart, and Howard Kirschenbaum, which appeared in H. Kirschenbaum and S. B. Simon (Eds.), *Readings in Values Clarification*. Minneapolis, Minn.: Winston Press, 1974. Used with permission.

summer program and were attended voluntarily by about 250 teachers, with no stipend. Following the completion of these sessions, all interested teachers were given an opportunity to apply for the summer workshop. The plan was to give priority to the schools that had at least three teachers applying for the workshop. These teachers would form the nucleus of a team, which could then present the strategies to other members of their staff during the next school year.

THE SECOND YEAR

Merrill Harmin and I led a second summer workshop held in August 1970. Eight Akron teachers who, a week prior to this, had been to an advanced value-clarification workshop in Canandaigua, New York, served as discussion leaders. Seventy-five teachers, representing a number of schools, attended. The workshop was coordinated by two secondary resource supervisors who had been involved in planning the original workshop. The stipend in this workshop as in all other summer workshops was $15.00 per day. In the fall of 1970, I returned for a weekend follow-up workshop, attended voluntarily by about fifty of the seventy-five summer participants. The teachers received no stipend for any of the follow-up workshops. Early in 1971, teachers who had attended previous workshops were asked to submit samples of work or examples of lessons using value clarification, identifying successes and failures to the Office of Curriculum and Instruction.

The plan at this time was to train a team of Akron teachers to assume some of the responsibility for workshop leadership. Ten teachers were selected and sent to the National Humanistic Education Center, in August of 1971, for advanced training. Upon returning, the team assisted Harmin in conducting the third summer workshop.

THE THIRD YEAR

Approximately three hundred teachers attended this third week-long, summer workshop. The ten team members worked as assistants to the leader in large group sessions during the morning. In afternoon sessions, the team worked as facilitators for smaller, grade-level or subject-matter groups. In the fall of 1971, Harmin and I returned to another follow-up weekend workshop. I remained in Akron the following week visiting the classrooms of the ten team members and meeting with administrators. The team, administrators, and I met to discuss the future role of value clarification in Akron. A plan for (1) value-oriented curriculum development; (2) a newsletter for the 400 to 500 Akron teachers who had been in a summer value-clarification workshop; (3) the formation of a demonstration school staffed by volunteer teachers from the summer workshops; and (4) further transferring of training responsibilities from the outside consultants to the Akron team of specialists was enthusiastically endorsed by the consultants, the team, and to a large extent by the administration. Owing to administrative problems and delays, however, the first three proposals were never actualized. In my opinion, this inability to move beyond the workshop stage to more concerted efforts on the part of the value-clarification "community" within Akron represented a major disappointment to, and a serious limitation of, the program.

On the other hand, the fourth proposal, the increasing responsibility for training undertaken by the Akron team, went ahead very successfully. The members were asked to submit a written personal evaluation of their strengths and weaknesses and their desire for future involvement with value clarification as specialists. In the spring of 1972, four of them (two elementary and two secondary teachers, three women and one man) were selected to serve as specialists for a fourth introductory workshop in the coming summer. A week was spent planning the workshop.

THE FOURTH YEAR

For the first time, the workshop was divided into two groups based on prior involvement. A beginning workshop for approximately 200 teachers was conducted by the four specialists, assisted by the other team members. Harmin conducted an advanced workshop for fifty teachers who had attended a beginning workshop in previous years. He also served as consultant to the specialists. The two workshops ran simultaneously in separate buildings.

PHYSICAL PLANT FOR WORKSHOPS

Each year the summer workshop has been in a different school. Among the factors considered important in selecting the site were: (1) accessibility; (2) rooms for large- and small-group activities; and (3) movable furniture. Materials were kept at a minimum—chart paper, magic markers, and index cards. Some audiovisual equipment was used. In addition to the stipend, each teacher was allocated a sum of money to purchase books and materials on value clarification.

EVALUATION

At the end of the summer workshops of 1971 and 1972, the participants were asked to fill out an evaluation form. In 1971, 209 teachers responded. In the overall rating of the workshop, 97.1 percent indicated that the workshop was "good" or "excellent." Over 94 percent indicated that they would welcome further training; 78 percent of this group indicated that they would be interested even without a stipend. In 1972, 239 teachers responded. There were about the same number of teachers from outer city schools as there were from inner city schools. The total showed that almost all felt the workshop was "good" or "excellent." Ninety-five percent indicated they were interested in further training, and most of them said they would attend without a stipend. In both years, 99 percent indicated they would use the strategies they had learned in their classrooms. The summary and conclusions for both 1971 and 1972 showed these comments:

"All respondents viewed the value-clarification workshop as extremely worthwhile."

"Workshops should be offered even if stipends are not available."

"Workshops should include representation of professional staff personnel (teachers, counselors, principals, and central office staff)."

"All teachers should attend a workshop on value clarification."

Comments also frequently mentioned were:

"In-service sessions throughout a school year should have the main theme of Value Clarification."

"More time should be spent working on grade levels, subject areas, and special areas, i.e., art, gym, music, etc."

CLASSROOM INVOLVEMENT

The impact made by the first group of teachers who attended a value-clarification workshop was subtle and appeared to lack impetus. A closer appraisal indicated, as with any pioneer effort, that progress was slowly but surely made in interesting other teachers in value clarification. The first efforts resulted in teachers in isolated situations using the strategies. As other teachers in their buildings listened and observed them, they became interested enough to ask questions. Since the spring of that year, when two of us returned to do an in-service training session for most of the district's professional staff, there has been a substantial increase each year in the number of teachers who have attended workshops. The pattern can be characterized as being "each one teach one."

Teachers at every grade level and from all sections of the city report enthusiastically about their use of value clarification in the classroom. In the early stages they found it difficult to make it a part of the regular classroom activities. Often, the strategies were presented as an activity to stimulate thinking in a very general way. As teachers became more skilled at using the strategies, a greater degree of sophistication emerged. Many teachers are now able to work with subject matter on three levels: (1) facts; (2) concepts; and (3) values. In many classrooms the experienced teacher has integrated value clarification with curriculum to such an extent that students no longer see strategies as isolated activities. A few examples may be useful.

One teacher was being cautioned by colleagues about a student he had received as a disciplinary transfer from an inner-city high school. The teacher was told "never to turn his back on the student." By the time the teacher received these warnings, the student had already been attending his classes for over a week. When the student first came into class, the other students automatically included him in their groups. One particular strategy, Validation, was very effective in making him feel part of the group. After a few days, he told the teacher that this was the first time anyone had ever paid any attention to what he did that was good. When slower students reach high school, many are afraid to respond because they have been "put down" so often by teachers. Students who have not been successful in the context of traditional educational approaches see value clarification as giving them an equal place in the classroom. They find that such humanistic interaction with teachers and students helps them develop an awareness of being capable, and lovable, too.

A high school boy who was cutting classes made an effort to attend his English class regularly. The teacher had developed a feeling of trust among her students through the use of value strategies. In one Value Sheet that this student completed, he told of stealing a television set from a friend. Later he reported his part in the theft to the authorities. Many teachers report that students exposed to value clarification become more accepting of one another. Value clarification also gives students an opportunity to see the human side of teachers. When a student becomes aware of the conflicts in a teacher's life, it legitimatizes his feelings about his own conflicts and gives him some support as he seeks solutions.

The classroom environment becomes more dynamic when value clarification is used. Teachers report that a more mobile and flexible program is developed. Students move from large-group arrangements to small groups as the need arises. Often a discussion period becomes more meaningful and open when three or four people share with one another. In one situation, in which a teacher was observing a Support Group (#79) discussion, she noticed one child who rarely said anything. Using a clarifying response, the teacher asked the child about this. The reply was: "I like to listen." This little girl was developing a very important communication skill.

During a Class Circle meeting, a teacher was using strategies to clarify conflicts that were of concern to the students. The school counselor was also a part of the group. As the children became more aware and involved with the interaction taking place, one little girl directed a question to the counselor: "Are you learning things from us?" A simple sentence revealing the insight of a young child who felt comfortable in asking an adult if he was clarifying his values.

An awareness of the group process following a class project was revealed to a third grade through some Unfinished Sentences. Children completed the phrase "Working in groups I . . ." Following are some of their responses:

"Working in groups I learned to get along."

"Working in groups I learned a lot about other people."

"Working in groups I learned that if I want to work, I can."

"Working in groups I learned working in groups is OK, but I like working by myself."

A kindergarten teacher draws faces that express moods, that is, a sad face, a happy face, an angry face, etc., on individual discs. She then uses an Unfinished Sentence, and the children turn up the face that expresses their feeling. If she says, "Snowy days make me . . . ," then each child turns up a disc reflecting his or her feeling about snowy days. The children are given an opportunity to state the complete sentence, building verbal skills as well as affective understanding. As the year progresses, the teacher includes sentences that confront issues that are very real to the small child. When children do not want their feelings known, they cover their faces after they turn them up. Others are quite open and check to see who agrees with them and who differs. At other times the children are asked not to use their discs, but to use their own faces to express feelings—more of a role-playing situation.

A counselor at the junior-high-school level uses value-clarification strategies when counseling groups of students who have been referred to him for disciplinary action. He helps them explore alternatives to the actions that got them in trouble and the consequences of each. Also, he gives the students the alternatives he has for dealing with them as offenders. They seek other possible alternatives and rank order the realistic ones. Each student makes a choice based on his understanding of the total process.

A secondary resource supervisor visits classrooms and observes the lessons for possible uses of value-clarification strategies. In a conference with the teacher she shows how the strategies might have been used. Hopefully, she has aroused the teacher's interest and a desire to attend a future workshop.

Since value clarification has been introduced to teachers in the Akron schools, special curricular areas have included the value-clarification technique as part of the overall program. Probably, the most extensive project is a new career-education program that includes every grade level, kindergarten through twelve. Value clarification is used by the teachers and counselors in the program to make the students aware of careers, work, and themselves.

A new course in behavioral science at the high-school level is being taught using value clarification and other humanistic education techniques. In the fall of 1972, one of the junior high schools was changed to a middle school. The teachers assigned to the school attended a value-clarification workshop. They report that using value-clarification strategies is an important part of lesson planning.

Another project, "Friends Across the City," involved two elementary classes—one from an inner-city and one from an outer-city school—who visited each other every month for a year. The students spent a whole day getting to know one another. The teachers used value-clarification strategies to bring about an awareness of themselves and others that destroyed many of their previously held racial myths and prejudices.

SPECIALISTS' ACTIVITIES

Value clarification has spread from workshops and classrooms into many other areas. Value-clarification specialists from Akron have been called on to demonstrate strategies for college classes and to talk to student/teacher seminars. The specialists and team members have done in-service programs within their own buildings and also for teachers in other buildings. As a part of the Trend project, an adult-education program in Akron, members of the team have taught mini-courses in value clarification to parents desiring it. Other school districts within the state have had in-service programs and workshops facilitated by the specialists. The specialists' involvement has also extended to workshops out of the state. Teachers, principals, and counselors from both in-state and out-of-state schools have come to observe value clarification in action in classrooms. College professors and church administrators have asked for and received permission to attend summer value-clarification workshops being taught in Akron. Presentations have been made to the Akron Board of Education, church groups, an honorary teacher's sorority, a group of administrators, counselors, supervisors, and school psychologists from northeast Ohio, and other interested community groups. Teachers as well as specialists have pre-tested materials to be published in the value-clarification area.

STRENGTHS

From the workshop evaluations come these statements:

"Value clarification teaches children how to think, make decisions, choose from among alternatives, get along with others, and better understand themselves and their world."

"Value clarification brings out the importance of listening."

"I now realize that living together happily depends on our listening and actively trying to understand people, and this is as important as teaching subject matter."

"I think I can teach my subject better through value clarification because it humanizes education and also humanizes the teacher."

"The strategies are easy to use and very flexible."

"The strategies expose children to ideas in ways that are new and interesting to them."

WEAKNESSES

Weaknesses expressed by teachers were:

"No set curriculum or study guides."

"Not enough representation of principals, counselors, resource teachers, and central office staff (administrators)."

"Vagueness of role of specialists in planning—past, present, future."

"More techniques should be demonstrated for teachers of special areas, that is, art, music, gym, etc."

"Groups should be smaller."

CONCLUSION

Value clarification has received strong support from the Central Office Administration and the School Board. It was the beginning of a trend to include more humanistic approaches to education in Akron. Changes in attitudes and student participation can be seen by visiting teachers in classrooms where value clarification is being used.

Since the beginning of value-clarification workshops in 1969, 651 teachers have attended at least one week-long summer session. Many have attended two or more workshops. These teachers have also attended weekend follow-up sessions on their own time with no pay, which indicates their degree of commitment.

In the future, Akron plans to continue involving teachers in beginning and advanced value-clarification workshops. Currently, many programs are being offered without stipends because funds are short in Akron as in many other cities. The story of value clarification in Akron does not end "and they lived happily ever after." The opposition to its use has been heard from some parents and teachers. But the professional manner in which it has been handled at all levels is the primary reason for the satisfaction expressed by many. Some of the weaknesses cited by teachers have been corrected. There have been many audiovisual materials and books on value-clarification strategies added to professional libraries. In-service meetings for special subject areas have been held to show how value clarification can be a part of the regular instructional program.

Principals are becoming more interested because they see the positive changes in students and teachers. However, supervision and follow-up in individual classrooms at this time [Spring 1973] is not available.

As the interest in humanistic education grows and develops, the use of value clarification will also continue to grow in Akron, Ohio.*

---

*My co-authors on this chapter were more optimistic than I was. It is my impression that not much has happened with value clarification in Akron since the summer 1974 workshop. I think our great contribution was in helping several hundred teachers learn to use value clarification. This skill, combined with their renewed enthusiasm and commitment and the many positive side effects indicated in the chapter, leave me thinking that the results were well worth the effort. A generation of students, thousands of them, will be better for it. However, I still believe what I thought in 1973, that our failure to move beyond individual change to system-wide coordination and structured change represents a major limitation of the training program.

PART III:

BUILDING VALUE CLARIFICATION INTO THE CURRICULUM

Chapter 9

TEACHING THE THREE-LEVELS THEORY OF SUBJECT MATTER

Whenever I work with school teachers, religious educators, drug abuse and human sexuality educators, and other content-oriented specialists, I am generally quite certain that one thing on their minds is: How does value clarification relate to my subject area?

These people may be quite open to the theory and strategies of value clarification, but unless they are made aware of specific connections between value clarification and their subject matter, they are certain to leave the session with the notion that value clarification is something that takes place on the side, during breaks in the study of subject matter. Therefore, I give top priority to introducing this audience to the three-levels theory of subject matter, as described in our book, *Clarifying Values Through Subject Matter* (Harmin, Kirschenbaum, & Simon, 1973). This chapter assumes the reader is familiar with the three-levels concept.

The type of introduction will vary with the length of my presentation. Following are some examples:

1. If I am doing a one- to one-and-one-half-hour demonstration of value-clarification strategies, as described in the previous section, I will simply mention the three-levels concept, saying something like: "Many of you are probably wondering how value clarification relates to the traditional subject areas you are responsible for teaching in your classrooms. Is value clarification entirely separate from subject matter, or can the two go hand in hand, and possibly even enhance each other? We believe the latter is the case, and we have developed a three-levels concept of subject matter that shows how any subject area can be taught on three levels—the fact level, the concept level, and the value level." If I do not have time to adequately explain the three-

levels theory, I at least like the people to know it exists and where they can go to learn more, if they wish to.

2. In a three-hour or one-day workshop with a school faculty, I will probably take about twenty minutes to describe the three-levels theory and maybe answer a few questions if there is time. I usually do it in one of two different ways.

In the first way, I take a topic of interest or of familiarity to most of the participants and show in detail the type of questions and issues that might be explored on the three different levels. The Thanksgiving story elaborated on in *Clarifying Values Through Subject Matter* is one I frequently use. Teaching the theory at a workshop in the Adirondack Mountains, I used examples of "teaching about the Adirondack Mountains with a focus on values." There usually is not time to have the participants respond to the questions, so it is a good idea just to present them as examples, putting some notes on the chalkboard or on newsprint ahead of time. This makes it easier for the teachers to follow and clearly visualize the three different levels. Again, I acknowledge that this one example does not do justice to all their different subject areas and that they should refer to the lists of materials for specific examples pertaining to their subject area.

In the second way, I briefly state several different subject areas as examples. I start by taking one or two minutes to explain what the fact level is. For example, I remind them of a couple of facts from the Pilgrim story (history), a couple of facts from digestion (science), a couple of facts from a Bible story (religious education), and one or two other areas. Then I briefly explain the concept level and just as briefly give them a couple of examples of concept-level questions or activities for each of the factual examples I gave earlier. Then I explain the value level and show how these same topics could be taught with a focus on values. This approach does not go into as much depth with one example as does the first approach, but it does give a broader idea of the way the theory works across different subject areas.

3. In a one- or two-day workshop, I often describe the theory as above and then do one of the following:

- I might invite the participants to ask me how I would teach a specific aspect of their subject on the value level. If I simply gave example after example myself, it would get quite boring; however, by having the participants almost challenge me to spontaneously come up with examples from their subject, some tension and excitement is created. But I must be very well grounded in the three-level theory and feeling reasonably loose and creative. This approach can work even better with team-teachers, since if one cannot come up with a good idea, the other can pitch in and help.

- In another approach, after presenting the theory with one extended example of my own, I ask some volunteers from the group to suggest a topic they are teaching now or about to teach on which they would like some help as to how it could be taught on all three levels. I solicit several topics and choose one that lends itself to examples. Then I ask the teacher to briefly describe some of the facts or concepts involved in the topic or unit so that everyone has a fairly good idea what the topic is about. Next, I ask the group to come up with some questions that this teacher might ask his or her students that will move the topic to the third level, or what activities he or she might have the class do. I give them about two minutes of time alone to think, and then I ask for ideas. I monitor the suggestions in terms of their relevance to each of the three levels; for example, I might say something like "I think that would be a good question on the *concept* level" (as opposed to saying, "I'm sorry, that's not a value-level question"). Beyond that I let the ideas flow, since it is more important that teachers come to understand what teaching on the third level is, than to be able to come up with excellent questions right away.

4. In two-day and longer workshops, I often set aside, near the end of the workshop, forty-five minutes to an hour of work time for participants to apply what they have learned to their back-home situations. I suggest they get together in subject-area groups or in grade-level or common-interest groups to do this. In these small-group discussions I encourage participants to use the third level, to find ways in which to use the strategies in connection with their subjects, to take a topic and ask third-level questions, and so on. (See Chapter 6 on designing a two-day workshop for further discussion of using these back-home focus work groups.)

5. All the examples given thus far of teaching the three-levels theory have assumed that this aspect of value clarification plays a relatively minor role in the workshop, that the major theory and strategies should get the bulk of the time. However, this may not always be the best approach. There are some groups—high school faculties, for example—that are so oriented toward subject matter that it might be wise to make this the major focus of a workshop or presentation. What follows, then, is a design for a one-hour presentation/

workshop, based on a similar one I learned from Merrill Harmin, in which subject matter is the entire focus; strategies are never even mentioned.

I begin by explaining, very briefly, the three-levels concept of subject matter, giving one extended example, such as the Pilgrim story. After describing and giving examples of the facts and concepts related to the Pilgrims, the teacher asks questions or suggests activities that help the students relate the subject matter to their own lives. They discover "what this has to do with *me*." They use the subject matter to develop and clarify their own values. I also give some examples of how a teacher could teach the Pilgrim story on the value level. I take no more than fifteen minutes to present this whole overview of the three levels.

At this point, I like to give participants a chance to try out this approach toward subject matter. I might do this by reading or telling them a story, reading an excerpt from a newspaper on some scientific discovery, playing a song from a record I brought with me, or showing them a picture. Working alone, participants are asked to write down a few fact-level questions, a few concept-level questions, and a few value-level questions they could ask about the material that was presented. Then I call on volunteers, asking for a few fact- and concept-level questions first, but spending a bit more time hearing their value-level questions. I keep this discussion moving along, being careful not to get bogged down analyzing or discussing any one question. I readily admit that sometimes it is hard to distinguish a concept-level from a value-level question, and I ask for as many examples of questions as there is time for.

Then I give them another example of a slightly different nature from the first one. Thus, if I gave them a literary example the first time, I might give them a scientific example the second time so that they can see that this approach works equally well for different types of subject areas. I repeat the procedure. If quite a few people have ideas they want to contribute, but there is not enough time to call on everyone, I might suggest that they take a minute each to talk with their neighbor about some of the ideas they came up with.

I close by explaining a bit more of what we are trying to do on the value level; that is, I briefly describe the valuing process and value clarification.

This little sequence can fit into any number of longer workshop designs. For example, having shown faculty members that you are aware of their subject-matter concerns, you can begin to introduce value-clarification strategies as further tools for teaching on the third level. There is no reason why this one-hour sequence could not be inserted whole into a one- or two-day value-clarification workshop. The facilitator could also move from this one-hour design to a lengthy process of building a three-levels curriculum. However, for a thorough examination of curriculum building, I prefer a more complete, integrative approach.

REFERENCE

Harmin, M., Kirschenbaum, H., & Simon, S. B. *Clarifying values through subject matter*. Minneapolis, Minn.: Winston, 1973.

Chapter 10

INTEGRATING VALUE CLARIFICATION INTO THE LARGER CURRICULUM: HOW TO BUILD UNITS AND COURSES

DEVELOPING A CURRICULUM MODEL

The most sophisticated use of value clarification is its integration into the curriculum, so that it is perceived as a natural part of the learning process rather than as a special activity that takes place apart from the study of subject matter. In order to accomplish the integration of value clarification into the curriculum in my own teaching, I developed a model of curriculum building that has wide application across grade levels and subject areas. For me, this model makes both the study of subject matter and the application of value clarification more effective. In this chapter, I will first describe the curriculum-development model and then discuss ways in which teachers may be trained to use it.

Lots of Paper

The first step is to get lots of paper. This process can often generate 100 to 200 teaching ideas, organized into several categories. It is important that you have plenty of room to think, to keep the categories separate, and to be able to clearly read your writing. I find that by spreading out over many sheets of clean paper, I think more effectively and creatively. A fresh sheet of paper seems to invite new ideas; a cluttered one seems to resist them.

What Is Worth Teaching?

This is a question I first heard asked by Sid Simon. It is so obvious it is often overlooked. As teachers, we are handed an anthology and told to "teach it." Our students must take standardized tests, so we teach for the tests: our teachers taught a certain way, and we teach the same way. But what is *worth* teaching?

This question is the first step of the curriculum-building model; that is, to discover what it is about our subject area that moves us so much we might proclaim, "*This* is worth teaching." Why did we become an English teacher, or science teacher, or math teacher in the first place? There must have been something about that subject that excited or interested us. What was it?

As an English teacher, for example, I was excited by the idea of using literature to get students to think about important ideas and issues and to be able to use writing as a way to clarify their values regarding those ideas and issues. Although I acknowledged the importance of building reading and writing skills, that was not what turned me on to English teaching—it was the *ideas*, the opportunity to have students reading, thinking, and talking about important issues—that is why I became an English teacher. So I ask myself: what ideas, in particular? What themes did I feel were most important and most interesting for my students to grapple with? The answers to that question provide the topics for the *thematic units* to be studied throughout the year. One year, for example, I selected two units, each lasting an entire semester. They were called "On Becoming a Person" and "Man and God." The process of how we develop our unique personalities and grow into adulthood, I thought, was a very exciting and important topic—one that the students could well appreciate, and one that is featured in many fine works of fiction and biography. I felt similarly about the "Man and God" theme. Another year, I divided the course into four thematic units—Alienation, Love, Race, and Religion.

Science teachers usually use this thematic approach. In biology, for example, there may be a unit on Digestion, Reproduction, Genetics, and so on. Other science teachers have departed from the traditional units and have created their own. One chemistry teacher, for example, asked herself: what are the important social issues today in which chemistry is an important factor? In this way she came up with four thematic units: Drugs, Pollution, Food, and Atomic Energy. She organized the entire year's study around those four themes.

So the first step in building the curriculum is to identify at least one theme worthy of the students' and your time. And the students can play a part in this decision. Their ideas on what they want to learn can help you build a curriculum with built-in student motivation. Thus, whether you have chosen the theme, or the students have, or it has been a joint decision, write the theme on the top of your first sheet of paper.

Cover Sheet: An Overview

Underneath the name of your thematic unit on the cover sheet write the following:

1. Readings
2. Audiovisuals
3. Resource people
4. Field trips
5. Fact, concept, and skill-building activities
6. Value clarification and other humanistic education activities
7. Assignments, projects
8. Action projects
9. Objectives
10. Requirements
11. Evaluation

Take the next eleven sheets of paper and head them accordingly. The cover sheet is your "table of contents" for the unit. It provides an overview of what you will be doing in your planning and helps you more easily to locate the right page as you need it. Now go on to the first page.

Readings

On this page, list all the readings you can think of that would seem to be a helpful part of your unit. If your course has a required text or anthology then list it here, but do not be limited by it. What else is there? Any books of yours at home? Anything in the school bookroom? What about articles you have seen, or periodicals? Poetry? Do not worry too much about reading level for now. Some students may be able to handle it, others will not. Later you can make such decisions as: Should I order this one for the whole class? Should this one be placed on a reading shelf in the back of the room? Should I hold this one aside and recommend it to specific students if they seem interested? Could I take these few pages and have them duplicated so each student can have a copy? Would the librarian make a "reserve" shelf for these items? And so on. But now you are brainstorming. Just keep going until you run out of steam. Then go on to the next page. Later, if another idea for a reading comes into mind, go back and put it down.

Keep in mind that readings (and audiovisuals and resource people) provide an excellent opportunity to expose students to alternative viewpoints. In the "Man and God" unit, for example, we read all of, or selections from, *Oedipus Rex*, the *Book of Job*, *Crime and Punishment*, the *Rubaiyyat of Omar Khayyam*, and *The Plague*, which represent a whole gamut of religious/metaphysical views from traditional/conservative to atheistic. A chemistry teacher doing a unit on atomic energy could, by the same token, bring in newspaper and magazine articles representing divergent views on the subject of atomic power plants. Value clarification can take place without once doing a value-clarification "strategy." It begins with the challenge of varying viewpoints, and reading is an excellent medium for creating this challenge.

Audiovisuals

What films do you know that fit into this theme? Which can be ordered? Which does the school own? Which are playing at local movie theaters? What about film strips? Tapes? Visual aids? Television, too, often provides excellent programs on a wide variety of subject matter. Look through the *T.V. Guide*. Are there any serial programs or specials that the students might watch that would touch on your theme? Put them all down on your list.

Resource People

Are there people you know or who you can find who have something to contribute to your study of this subject? Start with yourself. What knowledge, skills, or experience do you have that you would like to share? Are there other teachers in your building or district who could share their special backgrounds with your students and, thereby, contribute to the unit? What about the students' parents or the students themselves? Are there others in the community—business people, community leaders, people in the news, civil servants? Is there someone who might not come just to your class but who might be willing to address the entire school?

Some resource people who have visited my classes are author Joseph Heller (*Catch-22, Something Happened*), the school principal (who knows a lot about haiku poetry), two "hippies" (the students were writing a play about drug abuse at the time), black students from an inner-city school (we were a mostly white suburb), and a four-year-old child (to demonstrate some of Piaget's learning principles). Typically, it is much easier than one might imagine to receive positive responses to invitations from interesting people who can often provide some of the most unforgettable learning experiences of the year.

Field Trips

The list of "Resource People" consists of all the people who might come to you. On this page, the list should contain the names of people and places that your class might visit. Elementary school classes tend to do this more often, as with the obligatory trip to the firehouse. It is somewhat more difficult to arrange field trips with secondary classes, but it can be done. For the "Man and God" unit, for example, when the minister, priest, or rabbi could not come to us, we arranged to visit churches and temples. Chemistry classes can arrange to visit an atomic power plant, a sewage disposal plant, a chemistry laboratory, a pharmaceutical factory, and so on. The world beyond the school walls is filled with potential learning experiences.

Think big, you have nothing to lose. My English class was reading short stories by John Cheever. One girl (eleventh grade) looked up his number, called, asked if we could visit him at his home, and he agreed. In fact he was delighted!

Fact, Concept, and Skill-Building Activities

Dig into your storehouse of past experiences, your notes, and your creativity to list all the possible learning experiences you can think of to help your students learn the facts, concepts, and skills involved in your thematic unit. The lecture and the workbook may be included here, but go beyond them—role playing, laboratory work, inductive teaching, programmed instruction, simulations, good discussion questions, and so on. Make your notes specific, not general. For instance, list a specific discussion question that you have used or could use, a specific lecture that works especially well, a specific laboratory experiment, and so on.

Value Clarification and Other Humanistic Education Activities

Various items belong here. First, you might include "third-level" questions or activities to follow the facts and concepts learning that you have just recorded. These would be discussions or written questions or other activities that would help students personalize the information and ideas they have just explored.

At this point in my planning, I normally pick up a copy of the *Values Clarification Handbook* and glance at each strategy and ask myself, "Can this be used or adapted to fit my unit?" Ten to twenty of the strategies usually seem quite appropriate. Although I probably do not end up using them all, I write them down on the list.

I also look at several other handbook-type volumes in the humanistic education field. Keeping my subject area in the back of my mind, I leaf through them looking for new activity ideas.

Whether you have a collection of books or your own notebook of favorite learning experiences involving feeling, thinking, choosing, and communicating, search for the ones that might play a part in the unit. Again, do not write these down in general terms, but indicate the specific application you have in mind. For example, instead of writing down "rank order," write one or more specific rank orders that would apply to your topic.

Assignments, Projects

On this page you make a list of all the assignments or projects your students could become involved in. The "activities" section above covered mostly classroom activities. This section includes activities that are usually assigned for homework or ongoing group work in or out of the classroom. Here, as before, think of which assignments worked well in the past and new ones that will be even better. Try to think more broadly than just writing assignments, although some of these are fine. Think also in terms of group work, panels, debates, collages, surveys, library research, laboratory work, writing and performing a play, class magazine, conducting an assembly for the school, teaching younger children, interviewing parents and others; changing the classroom environment to fit the theme (bulletin boards, seating, lighting), and so on. Sensitivity Modules (#45) make excellent assignments and projects; I always check out that value clarification strategy in particular, to see if it would have any applications for my unit.

Note: Sometimes it is difficult to categorize an activity under one or another heading: Is it a "value-clarification activity" or an "assignment," for example. Do not be overly troubled by this. The categories are only there as a guide, to stimulate your thinking. Put the idea down wherever it seems to fit best. The important thing is to record it, so you do not forget it.

Action Projects

It is easy to focus on the prizing and choosing part of value clarification, the activities that involve *talking about* feelings, thoughts, and choices, and never get to the action stage, *doing* something concrete to demonstrate values. There are two ways I have focused on action in this curriculum-building sequence.

One way is to code my lists of "value clarification and other humanistic education activities" and "assignments, projects" by putting an "A" next to any of the activities that are action projects. If I do not see any "A's," then I take time to think of some action-oriented activities. In the "Man and God" unit, I asked my students what, if anything, they would like to do—differently or the same—as a result of their studying and thinking on this subject. I might even give an assignment with about five options from which they have to choose one; for example, attend a religious service of their choice and write a paper, write a letter to one of their former religious school teachers expressing their views on the strengths and weaknesses of their religious education, speak to their parents about . . ., etc. The chemistry teacher with the atomic energy unit could have her students write letters to a newspaper editor, congressperson, Ralph Nader, etc., expressing their views on the use of atomic power plants.

A second approach I sometimes use in this curriculum-development model is to allocate a separate page for action projects; I believe it is important enough to warrant its own category. Whichever approach one takes, the main thing is not to forget this dimension of the valuing process. In fact, an action project can easily become the main focus for the subject matter study. In a history course I once taught, in a unit on utopias, our class designed a utopian school and then tried to make it the reality. That action project necessitated much reading, writing, and public speaking, and a much deeper understanding of the subject than if the students merely had to answer test questions about utopias. The chemistry teacher with the unit on atomic energy, similarly could involve her class in an action project focused on opposing (or supporting, or one group for each) the construction of a new atomic power plant in the area; or in another of her units that year (on pollution, for example), she could have her students take samples of water from a nearby body of water, analyze the chemical content, and begin an action project, if needed, to clean up the city's waters. When students (or adults) are motivated by a desire to act upon their values, they learn much more about the subject matter because the subject matter is now relevant to their own goals and purposes.

Ask for Help

I like to begin this curriculum-development process myself, sitting at home, brainstorming all the good ideas I can think of. I have my memory, my notes and files, and, very likely, outlines of units similar to this one I have taught before. But once I run out of steam, I go in search of help. The question I ask is usually phrased something like "I'm doing a unit on _____; do you know of any _____ (readings, audiovisuals, resource people, field trips, activities, or projects) that would be good for my students?" I might ask that question of friends, colleagues, spouse, department chairman, principal, university professors, curriculum supervisors—anyone, professional or not, who might have even a single idea to contribute.

Ask Your Students

I have been proceeding here assuming that the teacher is the one who is making all the decisions and doing all the planning. Without going into the complicated issue of who should decide what goes on in a classroom, let me say the students can be a great help in this curriculum-development model. They have lots of ideas for readings, films, television programs, resource people, and the like, which you or I or our colleagues would never even think of. Soliciting their help can lead to a better unit, both in terms of motivation and available resources. If they feel that they have had a part in planning it, that it is *their* unit, they are more likely to become willingly involved. And they can bring in books and magazines to share and suggest activities that will not only enhance the unit for *them*, but that will also give *you* good ideas for your future lists.

Some teachers involve the students in the process from the beginning, serving mostly as a facilitator while letting them do most of the work. The first decision would involve selecting a theme for the unit. Here the teacher might offer some alternatives, the students might add theirs, and the selection would be made. Then the chalkboards around the room, or newsprint on all the walls, would be readied, so that student recorders could write down ideas as fast as they come from the class. The teacher could add his or her ideas, too. In this way, in a short time, students can develop their own curriculum, which might then be studied by the class as a whole or by individuals or small groups selecting their readings, field trips, and so on from the wide assortment available. This is much more productive than the laissez faire approach that says to students, "Well, what do you want to learn?" and gives no guidance in helping them identify and organize their learning resources.

Objectives

It may seem odd that the discussion of objectives has been left until nearly the end of this sequence. Usually, we think in terms of getting clear about our objectives and then finding the means to accomplish those goals. Here I have reversed the process.

Actually, most teachers have at least some idea of their objectives at the outset. There are some criteria operating, even if they are not clear or explicit. There is, of course, value in making vague criteria clearer. But I find that if this is done too early, it often stifles the curriculum-development process. Ask a group of teachers to specify their objectives in concise terms and they are likely to become defensive and resistant. This is hardly the frame of mind that will help them to develop new and exciting curricula.

I prefer to start differently, by opening doors, by encouraging divergent thinking, by tapping the teacher's inherent motivation or love for his or her subject area. If some of the items on the lists are later found to be irrelevant to the objectives, they can always be crossed off. The wealth of practical, usable, relevant ideas that are generated will be well worth the time it takes to cross off the few that are not. This curriculum-development model should be a rewarding process. I've seen teachers practically bouncing in their seats just thinking of all the exciting activities and readings and projects they can use with their students. That is what teaching is all about—someone who is excited about a book or an idea or an activity sharing it with someone else. I feel very strongly that if we lose this sense of teaching, all the clear objectives in the world will not amount to very much significant learning.

But there is a time to reflect on our goals, too, and for me, this seems about the right time for that. I find it helpful to divide this page into three sections, or to devote a separate page to each. These sections are *knowledge, skills,* and *attitudes.* (Sometimes I use a fourth category—*behavior change.*)

The first section asks this question: "What facts or concepts do I want my students to *know* as a result of this unit?" So I write down some of the major facts or concepts that seem basic to the subject. Then I ask, "What skills do I want them to learn, what do I want them to be able to *do,* once this unit is over?" And I note these. Finally, "What attitudes do I hope to foster?" And I note these. In the back of my mind, I continue to reflect on the questions with which I began my planning: "What is worth teaching? What of importance about this unit do I want my students to take away with them? In ten years from now, what about this unit will the students remember; what will have made a difference?"

I work on this for a while, but when it begins to get very tedious, I move on. I come back to this later, as I do with all the pages.

Requirements

Once I have a good idea of the range of activities and materials I may be using, and a greater clarity about my objectives, my next question is "What will I require of my students?"

Any teacher's requirements will vary depending on his or her teaching philosophy, students, subject area, and so on. In any case, it is important to be clear on just what your requirements are. How much reading and writing will be required? What about class participation and attendance? Will there be choices for the students as to how they meet the requirements? Can some students work independently in the library and still meet the requirements? What other options are there? By first looking at the curriculum and the objectives, you will be more likely to recognize that requirements are a means to an end and can vary from unit to unit and from student to student. The important thing is that the objectives be gained. Requirements should be appropriate to these.

I find that as I get clearer about what I want to ask of the students, I can communicate it more clearly to them, often in advance. This helps them get a realistic picture of what lies ahead so that they can plan their work more efficiently. It also gives students a chance to suggest alternative ways of meeting the requirements.

Evaluation

Sometimes evaluation methods help teachers achieve their objectives, and often they do not. I use this page to ask myself the following kinds of questions: If I use a traditional grading system—awarding "A" through "F," for example—is that going to help create the climate, the skill learning, the value clarification, the self-motivated action projects, and so on that I want in this unit? What will the positive and negative consequences be? How can I best introduce the evaluation procedure so as not to turn the class into a "me vs. them" situation? Should I discuss with the class several evaluation alternatives and see if we can reach a group decision? There are certain things, such as value-clarification activities, that I do not want to grade. But if they are not graded, then students tend to regard them as less important. How can I avoid that pitfall? Several of my students have not been motivated by grades in the past and there seems little likelihood that they will be now. Can I come up with a different evaluation system for them that might be more effective? And so on. This is a very complicated issue, yet I find that when I carefully consider it in the context of a specific unit, I can often come up with better ways to solve the problems of grading and evaluation. (See Kirschenbaum, Simon, & Napier, 1971, for a discussion of grading and evaluation alternatives.)

The Second Time Around

By the time I have finished my first round of planning, I have dozens of specific ideas for my unit, as well as a clearer picture of my objectives, requirements, and means of evaluation. Then I ask help from friends, colleagues, students, and others, as discussed earlier. And as new ideas occur to me, I add them to the appropriate lists.

Perhaps a week or so later, if I have left enough time, I thoroughly go over my lists again, putting down any new ideas that have come to me or that I may have heard during the week, and I think about any possibilities I may have missed. This does not mean I cannot add more ideas later, but now that I am ready to start organizing this mass of possibilities, I want to make certain I have as much information as I can gather before I begin the next stage.

ORGANIZING THE CURRICULUM

How do you take this plethora of possibilities and turn it into a day-to-day reality that is going to guide the energies of many people for several weeks, months, or even a whole year? How do you move from a hundred or more alternatives to selection, sequencing, and structuring, consistent with your overall objectives? Here I feel a bit like a comedian who has been telling a terrific joke and then forgets the punch line. There is no formula.

I personally have used this process to build curriculum for English and history courses in public schools and for at least four different college courses. I have seen it used by teachers on every different level and in many subject areas. And yet, when you get to this point, there is no one right way to proceed. However, I do have some suggestions from my own and from others' experience. I would caution the reader here that this part of the process is neither easy nor fun. It is a lot of hard work, but it yields valuable results.

Selection

Leland and Mary Martha Howe (1975) offer one suggestion that can be of some help here. They suggest making a chart, with all the objectives listed down the left-hand side and all the possible activities, assignments, readings and so on listed along the top. For each activity, reading, and so on, you then go down the column and put a check mark next to any of the objectives that that activity helps to achieve. The chart helps you easily identify which activities meet several of the objectives, which meet none of the objectives, which objectives have several activities to help achieve them, which objectives would not be met because there are no readings or activities that are checked on that line, and so on. This type of analysis takes a bit of time, but it helps tie the activities to your objectives. Even if you use another method of building your overall curriculum, this step can be a useful one to do later, to set your curriculum out in terms someone else, such as a supervisor or principal, can understand. In any case, the chart can help you select the curricular elements most consistent with your objectives. Personally, this chart approach is not my style. I think I tend to do this step in my head, keeping my objectives (as I listed them earlier) in the back of my mind and selecting the ones that seem most useful for achieving them. For those who take the time to work on this step, though, it can be a very helpful tool for selecting, explaining, or justifying the various parts of your curriculum.

Organizing

Whether I have used the chart method or my own intuition for selecting activities, I still have the bigger problem of how to organize them. The first thing I do toward this end is to stare at my lists for a long time. I think, I wonder, I fantasize a particular activity and how it might work; I think about a film on my list; I wonder if I should lay out all the requirements at the beginning or give them one at a time; I think about particular students I had last year and whether they would be able to read a particular book on my list; I notice how a particular assignment would go very well after a particular reading; I get anxious because the task seems so overwhelming; I wonder if we have enough copies of that paperback in the bookroom; I think to myself that this particular value-clarification strategy would be a very good way to begin the unit; I think of another activity that didn't work so well last year; I think that I should save this book until near the end of the unit and also this project, which would be a good way to tie the unit together; in fact, we could take a whole week for the students to present their projects to the class; on the other hand we could do it in one day if they set the projects up around the room and walked around and looked at each other's; and so on and on.

Through the concentration, the anxiety, and the confusion that results, small insights begin to appear. One by one, I make connections, see ways to sequence activities, further select and reject particular ideas, clarify my objectives—in short, organize my curriculum. What happens next? I have seen at least six different patterns emerge. I might use one exclusively, or I might use two or more of these approaches.

1. *Continue to contemplate.* I may just continue this process as I've described it. A little at a time, the curriculum organizes itself. I fill in my plan book or calendar. I rearrange things. I realize that I do not have any activities to achieve a certain skill-training objective, so I make a change to allow for that. I stick with it. I go back to it another

day. Eventually, my curriculum is complete, although of course, I may change it once it is actually in operation.

2. *Start at the beginning.* Once I have contemplated for a while, once several insights and sequences and decisions have emerged, I may decide to get very specific by starting from the first day; in other words, "What is the best thing I can do to actually begin the unit?" I look over my list. Maybe I find a value-clarification strategy, a film, a guest speaker—in any case, I make a tentative decision and put it down on my calendar or paper or plan book. Then I say, "Should there be an assignment that night following this introduction to the unit?" If so, I put that down. Then I ask myself: "Where will they be the next day? What would be just right to pick up and move forward from where we left off?" I look over my lists. Often I do not see anything that is appropriate, so I stop and create an activity or think of a reading or experiment or whatever that will fill that particular need. And so the curriculum unfolds. I start at the beginning and proceed this way right through to the end. Then I go back over it, check to see if I have been consistent with my objectives; see where I might further improve the selection and sequence; and keep polishing it until I am fairly satisfied with the overall design.

3. *Play it by ear.* Sometimes I decide to play it by ear. I go in with the first week planned, maybe even only the first day, and see how things go. I have more or less memorized my lists, so at the appropriate time I can suggest a reading or an activity, I can bring in a tape I have, I can give the assignment—all at just the right moment. Some teachers can do this very well. They may have done a great deal of preparation, but simply choose not to structure the curriculum beforehand. They want to see how it goes first, to see how the students react. They are able to teach spontaneously. I once suggested to a teacher that he "play it by ear" and he replied, "Yes, but what if I don't have your ear?" In other words, some teachers are simply not comfortable operating in this way. They would prefer to have the curriculum outlined beforehand and then feel free to depart from it if need be. Sometimes when I decide to play it by ear, it is a conscious pedagogic choice; other times it means I just have not left enough time for preparation, and I really have no choice. But it is a viable alternative, with pros and cons.

4. *Impose a time structure.* Often, in doing this kind of planning, I get a bit overwhelmed by all the possibilities and find it helpful to impose a structure on the week. I may decide, for example, that on Mondays I will give a lecture and conduct a class discussion, on Tuesdays have value-clarification experiences, on Wednesdays do skill-building activities, on Thursdays have students give reports and

conduct the class, on Fridays have them work on independent study projects. The chemistry teacher with the atomic energy unit might show films on Monday, lecture and ask questions on Tuesdays, conduct a demonstration experiment on Wednesdays, have independent laboratory work on Thursdays, and have small groups working on their action project on Fridays.

This is certainly an imposed structure in that the Monday discussion may be so good that it is more natural to continue it the next day than to go on to the Tuesday value-clarification exercises. And, in fact, a teacher using this type of structure may want to modify it from time to time to allow for such situations. But I believe there can be a great deal of value to such a structure, when the structure is viewed as a means to an end. If it increases the likelihood that the objectives will be achieved, it is useful. If it becomes structure for its own sake, it becomes self-defeating.

There are other types of structures. Dividing a whole year's work into four major units is a structure. A given unit, for example, could be divided into three parts. First would be input. Here the students would read, listen, visit, take tests, and so forth, all geared to help them understand the facts and concepts of the unit. The second part would involve their value clarification—discussions, activities, simulations—to help them think about the subject, write about their views, get in touch with their feelings, state their positions, and so on. The third part would have them involved in action projects or independent study projects in which they would further pursue their interest or their commitment by engaging in some type of project that would combine their knowledge of the subject with their own values. This structure has advantages and disadvantages; it may not be the best one for a given unit. But the point is to try to find structures that will enhance the unit and help achieve the objectives.

5. *Use the open classroom model.* I can utilize all my ideas in the form of an open classroom. I can bring in the books and filmstrips, schedule the films for certain days (posting this information on the bulletin board), set up a reading corner and a discussion corner. I can post charts with lists of suggested resource people, field trips, and so on. I can offer myself as a resource person and indicate, on the bulletin board, when I would like to offer certain lectures, value-clarifying experiences, and so forth. And, very important, I must make my requirements explicit so that students will know what is expected of them. Then they are on their own. They can listen to my lecture or not. They can work in whatever part of the room they wish (one requirement may be that no one can disturb someone else). They can work in the school library. They can organize field trips, and I will be happy to

help, perhaps going with them or helping to arrange for a parent to go with them. I am involved and interested in each person's work, but I respect the students' right to choose how they spend their time. I may use class meetings, learning contracts, evaluation folders, or any other structures that help open education work. I may use this system for part of the week or the whole week. It is an alternative available to most teachers, though it is not usually apparent.

6. *Have the class plan together.* As I suggested earlier, the students can do this whole process themselves, with some facilitation on the teacher's part. Look back to the section on "Ask Your Students." It suggests an alternative to the open classroom but still utilizes student self-directed learning.

Summary

Although these six approaches may seem easy enough on paper, each requires a great deal of hard thinking and careful planning. The results, however, are almost always a curriculum that is more fun to teach, more fun to experience, and more likely to achieve significant learning goals.

TEACHING THIS MODEL

I take teachers through this curriculum-development process much the same way I took the reader through it in this chapter. I make sure they have lots of paper. I ask them to select a theme or topic to work with. I have them work in pairs, if possible, so they can share ideas with one another. (Teams could work together, too, although I have never tried that approach.) I ask them to head one page "Readings" and to list several readings they can think of. I allow them only a few minutes. (There is not enough time to develop their entire curriculum in the workshop setting, but they can start the process and complete it later. They will have experienced enough of it to know how it works.) Then I have them head a page "Audiovisuals" and give them another few minutes to jot down ideas. They can go back to "Readings" if new ideas occur. (Sometimes I have them work alone for two minutes and then share ideas with their partner for two minutes.) I take them page by page through the process and describe the options for organizing the curriculum.

CONCLUSION

Although the title of this chapter is "Integrating Value Clarification into the Larger Curriculum," you will note that I have not used the term "value clarification" much at all. That is what I mean by integration. It is present throughout, but it does not depend on continual strategies. Reading and discussing alternative viewpoints, occasional strategies, writing assignments with value foci, action projects—this is the kind of value clarification that does not grow stale, that can be repeated year after year. It is not a new fad. It is education.

REFERENCES

Howe, L., & Howe, M. M. *Personalizing education: Values clarification and beyond*. New York: Hart Publishing, 1975.

Kirschenbaum, H., Simon, S. B., & Napier, R. WAD-JA-GET? *The grading game in American education*. New York: Hart Publishing, 1971.

PART IV:

VALUE CLARIFICATION: PAST, PRESENT, AND FUTURE

Chapter 11

A BRIEF PERSONAL HISTORY OF VALUE CLARIFICATION

For historical interest, and because teachers of value clarification should be familiar with its background, I would like to briefly describe the history of this approach. More important, this look into the past will provide a foundation for the following discussion of the present and future status of value clarification. Because I have felt myself to be a part of this "movement," my perspective of the history of value clarification is that of an insider looking out, rather than an outsider looking in. Thus, this is mainly a personal history, rather than an objective historical account, of the development of value clarification.

Value clarification (or *values* clarification) began with Louis Raths, a teacher/educator at Ohio State University and New York University who was very much influenced by the work of John Dewey. Raths recognized the importance of working with values, identified the behaviors or expressions that indicated a value or the lack of a value, and developed the notion of seven criteria for a value; that is, in order for something to be called a value it must meet the following seven criteria: (1) be chosen from alternatives, (2) be chosen after thoughtful consideration of consequences, (3) be chosen freely, (4) be prized and cherished, (5) be publicly affirmed, (6) be acted upon, and (7) be acted upon repeatedly and consistently.[1] Raths encouraged his students to use these processes to develop their own values. Kimball Wiles (Raths, Harmin, & Simon, 1966) recalled how Raths did this:

> Years ago when I was in graduate school Louis Raths intrigued me with his reactions to my comments. As far as I could detect he never really approved any statement I made. He would ask a question, make a non-

---

[1] Actually, Raths identified only five processes; Simon and Harmin urged the inclusion of two more.

committal observation, test my assertion by supplying additional data, ask if I had considered a different alternative. The experience was disconcerting to me. My previous educational experience had led me to expect to use the teacher as a means of determining the correctness of my answers. He was the person who knew and his role was to keep me informed of my progress in the search for truth. He was to provide reinforcement. And this teacher did not! I expected positive affirmation and support. And I received more questions and the expectation that I would continue to probe. (p. vii)

Although he did employ several of what later came to be called structured value-clarifying "strategies," including the Value Sheet, Raths' use of the clarifying response was his main vehicle for value clarification. Under Raths' direction, there was an early interest in research on the approach, and much of the research utilized the clarifying response in what was similar to a counseling situation.

Two doctoral students of Raths, Merrill Harmin and Sidney B. Simon, were very impressed by this style of teaching and went on to develop some new strategies in their own work as public school teachers and then as college teachers. Then, in the early sixties, they began to teach summer workshops and courses utilizing the value-clarifying methodology; however, the workshops were not yet called "value-clarification workshops." I remember how, in the summer of 1965, I visited a friend who was taking a three-week "human relations workshop" with Harmin and Simon at Rutgers University. At the time, there was lots of practice on the clarifying response and on creating value sheets.

In 1966, Raths, Harmin, and Simon's book *Values and Teaching* appeared and drew together the work that the three of them and their students had been doing over the previous years. This volume, for six years the only major publication on value clarification, served and still serves as a basic text on working with values in the classroom. Ironically, while value clarification is sometimes criticized today as having a weak theoretical and research base, *Values and Teaching* was generally acclaimed for its thoughtful, theoretical presentation and its interest in research, as well as its clear presentation of practical classroom methods.

As Raths reached retirement age and began to curtail his teacher-training activities, Harmin and Simon were increasing theirs, leading week-long or two-week-long summer workshops and giving occasional speeches or presentations during the school year.

The first workshop I team-taught with Harmin and Simon was in the summer of 1968. In 1969, the three of us printed our first flyer, a single page that advertised two week-long value workshops (one in

Rochester, New York, and the other in Philadelphia), the first advanced value workshop in Canandaigua, New York, and a human relations workshop in the Adirondack Mountains. We called ourselves "Values Associates," which, until it dissolved in 1974, served as a useful association for coordinating and disseminating new work on value clarification.

Although *Values and Teaching* was being adopted by an increasing number of college education courses, the approach was still not widely known. Until 1971, value clarification had been taught primarily in college courses or in week-long or longer summer workshops. My colleagues and I began to wonder if the model could not be adapted to a weekend workshop format and, thereby, reach a wider number of people throughout the year. So, for the spring of 1971, we scheduled three weekend workshops, one in Washington, D.C., one in Chicago, and one in Boston. We also put out a real brochure this time, announcing and describing the three spring and four summer workshops. The weekend workshops were successful, both in terms of attendance and in terms of how participants were able to transfer their learnings back to their school or home settings. We had been worried that we could not do enough in a weekend to enable people to use the approach back home. But the feedback we got indicated that there did not seem to be much of a difference between the transfer from a week-long workshop and the transfer from a weekend workshop. If there was a small loss with the weekend format, it seemed to be offset by the much larger number of people who could be reached through weekend workshops in their own areas. That fall, we scheduled six more weekend workshops in other locations. The next year, there were eight in the spring and eight in the fall. Whereas in 1970 we were reaching slightly more than a hundred people a year through workshops, by 1972 the number had grown to about two thousand.

A second development in 1971 was related to my leaving Temple University and moving to upper New York State to form the Adirondack Mountain (now the National) Humanistic Education Center. The center published a list of materials on value clarification, including reprints of articles we had written applying value clarification to English, history, math, science, and other areas. Until this point, enthusiastic workshop participants had difficulty finding materials. Most book stores did not stock *Values and Teaching* (they still do not), and few people had the time or the desire to hunt up articles in the library. By making available these books and materials to thousands of people who would use them and pass them on to colleagues, the theory and techniques of value clarification quickly and widely spread throughout the country.

The following year, the number of workshops increased, and, more important, Simon, Howe, and Kirschenbaum's book *Values Clarification: A Handbook of Practical Strategies for Teachers and Students* was published. Now the approach spread like wildfire. Workshop participants, armed with the *Handbook*, could more effectively bring their learnings back home and put them to work. The *Handbook* also made the approach easier to teach and to show one's colleagues. And, of course, for better or worse, one no longer needed to come to a workshop to gain access to value-clarification strategies. The philosophy and strategies quickly found their way into many different settings and helping professions—schools, religious education, scouting groups, families, social work, counseling, and so on.

The annotated bibliography at the end of this volume documents the growing number of publications on value clarification that followed publication of the *Handbook*. Workshop offerings also increased, with many new trainers and facilitators providing experiences in value clarification. Now value clarification is often cited as one of the two major approaches to value education, the moral-development approach of Kohlberg and associates being the other (although both these approaches are still less common than the indoctrination-moralizing approach).

It is apparent that the publications and training workshops in value clarification have changed their emphasis. The earlier focus emphasized the theory-research part of value clarification and utilized the clarifying response and the value sheet as the two main value-clarification strategies. It is significant that *Values and Teaching* devoted sixty pages to these strategies alone, compared to fifty pages that described eighteen other methods. We might call the clarifying response and the Value Sheet the "main strategies" and the other, repeatable, strategies, such as Voting and Continuum, the "bread-and-butter strategies." The *Values Clarification Handbook* also introduced a third type of strategy—the "one-time strategy"—as well as many new bread-and-butter strategies. One-time strategies, such as Fallout Shelter Problem (#48), Suitcase Strategy (#78), Alligator River (#50), Life Line (#53), and Obituary (#56) are generally done only once in a group's life. The focus on implementing value clarification, then, has seemed to move from the main and the bread-and-butter strategies to the bread-and-butter and the one-time strategies.[2]

Another development has been the growing number of applications of value clarification to various content areas. In a series of arti-

---

[2]In my own training efforts, I try to shift the emphasis back to the main and the bread-and-butter strategies.

cles by Harmin, Simon, and myself and in our *Clarifying Values Through Subject Matter* (1973), we used the facts-concepts-values concept of subject areas to show how the traditional pursuit of knowledge can be integrated with the search for values. The annotated bibliography details many more examples of how others have furthered this effort and moved into new areas of application. Leland and Mary Martha Howe (1975), for example, have developed a model for integrating value clarification with other approaches. Roland and Doris Larson's *Values and Faith* (1976) has applied value clarification to the religious education field. Many other examples of excellent new applications could be given.

Finally, we are seeing a renewed interest in theory and research in value clarification. The interest in theory comes in part from a defensiveness that many value-clarification trainers experience when confronted by the questions or objections of theoreticians. It seems that the more popular value clarification becomes, the more it is subject to such theoretical scrutiny. The renewed interest in research comes from many doctoral students who have been excited by value clarification and who are also looking for a dissertation topic and from drug-education programs utilizing value clarification and needing empirical support to maintain their funding. (See Chapter 3 for a discussion of these developments and the dozen or more new studies on value clarification.)

In this brief, personal history of value clarification, I have tried to highlight the various developments without evaluating them. But what does this history mean? What implications has it for the training and qualifications of value clarification? How can value-clarification trainers work together to advance the approach in the most effective manner? Where does value clarification go from here? What future developments may be predicted and even encouraged? These questions are the focus of the next two chapters.

REFERENCES

Harmin, M., Kirschenbaum, H., & Simon, S. B. *Clarifying values through subject matter*. Minneapolis, Minn.: Winston Press, 1973.

Howe, L., & Howe, M. M. *Personalizing education: Values clarification and beyond*. New York: Hart, 1975.

Larson, R., & Larson, D. *Values and faith*. Minneapolis, Minn.: Winston Press, 1976.

Raths, L. E., Harmin, M., & Simon, S. B. *Values and teaching*. Columbus, Ohio: Charles E. Merrill, 1966.

Simon, S. B., Howe, L., & Kirschenbaum, H. *Values clarification: A handbook of practical strategies for teachers and students*. New York: Hart, 1972.

Chapter 12

QUALIFICATIONS FOR VALUE-CLARIFICATION TRAINERS

As value clarification began to gain momentum and many new people entered the field as trainers, my colleagues and I frequently wondered whether we should establish a structured training and certification procedure for trainers in this field.

Sometimes urgings to start a training program came from students, colleagues, or participants who encouraged us to systematize and control the spread of value clarification in this way. Sometimes our inner promptings moved us in this direction. We asked ourselves whether we had a responsibility to see that value clarification was disseminated in the most responsible and most effective manner possible.

We were well aware of other individuals and groups who were involved in worthwhile work and who had chosen to control their "product" in a very businesslike fashion. Thomas Gordon's Effectiveness Training Associates, Palomares and Bissell's Human Development Institute ("Magic Circle"), the National Training Laboratories, and other organizations had developed franchise systems, training courses, certification procedures, or other carefully designed methods of managing their operations. Quality and financial control were two clear benefits.

However, this path was not our choice. Several factors entered into our consideration. First, we had no desire to "hold on to" value clarification. This fact was clear in our decision to publish the *Values Clarification Handbook* with its seventy-nine strategies. We wanted to give value clarification away, to see it used by the widest group possible, to teach people the philosophy and methodology and then have them use it, adapt it, change it, and apply it in any number of new ways and situations.

144

Second, the idea of certifying value-clarification trainers seemed impractical and self-defeating. Assuming we came up with a method of training and certification, once a person was a "certified" value-clarification trainer, he or she would become a representative of the whole value-clarification "movement." As such, it would be very important for that person to lead only "pure" value-clarification experiences. He or she could not conduct a workshop using any of the other approaches, such as techniques from group dynamics, counseling, personal growth, nonverbal activities, Parent Effectiveness Training, and so on. Otherwise the trainer might confuse the public as to what value clarification is and what it is not. Furthermore, although we might be able to distinguish a qualified value-clarification trainer from a non-qualified one, we would have no way of knowing who was qualified in group dynamics, counseling, personal growth, and so on. Thus, since they might *not* be qualified in these other areas, we could not permit other approaches to be integrated with value clarification.

This whole process contradicted everything we believed about good training. To make a value-clarification workshop work, it is essential that trainers understand and utilize other approaches that facilitate learning. Trust-building activities, group-process work, communication exercises often fit very well with value clarification and sometimes are required in order that value clarification be effective at all. If a requirement for doing value-clarification work were doing it in its "pure" form only, then my colleagues and I would be the first to flunk the requirement. We wanted to see value clarification grow in its variety and versatility and to find ways to integrate it with other useful approaches. We saw Parent Effectiveness Training, Magic Circle, and other excellent approaches as being limited by the necessity of having to be taught in isolation. The benefits of controlling value clarification were not worth the price of stultifying it.

Finally, there would be a personal price to pay. We want to spend our time developing new ideas and growing ourselves. The time and energy needed to develop and administer a certification program, we thought, would take us too far in a very different direction.

However, while we chose not to exert any quality *control* over value clarification, we still wanted to exert some quality *influence* in the field, if possible. In late 1973, I drafted a letter that Sid Simon, Merrill Harmin, and I signed and sent to individuals who were interested in or who were already conducting training in value clarification. This letter has been distributed as widely as possible. In it we summarized our thinking about the question of control and certification and presented our list of "Recommended Qualifications for Value-Clarification Trainers." With only a few changes, the following criteria or qualifications (directed at everyone who conducts workshops in value clarification or who trains others to use the value-clarification approach) are taken directly from that letter.

1. Participate in a two-day or longer workshop conducted by an experienced value-clarification trainer. Reading about value clarification is no way to learn the approach. Only when you experience the strategies, especially in a group setting with an effective facilitator, do you recognize their potency and realize how to lead experiences in this manner.

2. Use the value-clarification approach with a back-home target group—your students, your friends, groups with whom you work. When you have experienced success with value clarification, when you can say to others, "I've used it, it works, I know from my experience that such and such problems often occur and here is how I dealt with them; here is how I have adapted some of the strategies . . . ," you are likely to have much more legitimacy in others' eyes, and you will feel more confident and be more flexible and effective. We are uncomfortable with the idea of people experiencing a good value-clarification workshop and then starting to teach the approach to others before validating it in their own experience.

3. Read the literature. There has been a surprising amount of material written on value clarification. In addition, read about other approaches to value education and moral development.

4. Take an advanced value-clarification workshop. At this point, the only such workshops we know of are those offered by the National Humanistic Education Center and the Philadelphia Center for Humanistic Education.

5. Experience other workshops in the humanistic education field. There are many skills necessary for conducting value-clarification workshops other than knowing how to use value-clarification strategies. Laboratories in personal growth, communications, human relations, and organization development all contribute skills and understandings that are very helpful in conducting value-clarification workshops. In a value-clarification workshop, when some participants seem hostile, when subgroups begin forming, when open conflict breaks out, when someone bursts into tears, when all sorts of unpredictable human situations arise, your wider background in group dynamics and communication can mean the difference between a successful workshop and one that is characterized by chaos and confusion.

6. Be sure that you *believe* in value clarification and use it in your own life. This may seem so obvious that it need not be mentioned. On the contrary, we think it is a point that deserves special emphasis.

We use rank orders in our own lives. We are continually asking each other, our spouses, and our friends value-clarifying questions. We frequently think in terms of continuums. If you only practice value clarification in workshops, we hope you will not train others in this approach. Value clarification is not a series of games and gimmicks. It is a flexible, helping response that is applicable to a broad spectrum of human situations. In our experience, the person who has not discovered this is a less effective trainer than the person who has.

7. Pace yourself. Do not begin with a five-day workshop. Start with a shorter demonstration, and only as you become more experienced attempt longer, more intense workshops.

8. Always use feedback tools in your initial workshops and continue to use them frequently. Your best teachers may be your students. When you have finished, ask the group members to take ten minutes to help you, by writing down what they liked and what they did not like and what recommendations they would make if you did such a workshop again. Or use whatever device or questionnaire you may devise. There is probably no better way for you to get a realistic picture of yourself and your work and to develop further goals for your own improvement.

9. Hand out some type of list of materials at your workshops. We have found that if we simply list the titles of books and articles on the board at workshops, busy teachers rarely take the time to copy them down and then go in search of them. However, if participants are furnished with a printed list, including places where they can write for material, this is much more helpful, and many do follow up and obtain the materials.

10. Join a network or support group of others working with value-clarification methods and materials. This may be a local support group with your own colleagues or a wider association, like the Humanistic Educators Network sponsored by the National Humanistic Education Center, which sends its members periodic mailings containing articles, research, teaching methods, and other information on value clarification and other complementary approaches.

In summary, I urge all value-clarification trainers to meet these ten standards or qualifications. It is not necessary that all ten be completed before beginning to conduct short workshops or demonstrations, but the principle is that as people get deeper into training others in the value-clarification approach they will seek out experiences that maximize their continued growth and increased effectiveness. These ten "qualifications" are strong recommendations for those who want to go further in this area.

Chapter 13

THE FUTURE OF VALUE CLARIFICATION

At a recent International Conference on Values Education in Toronto, Milton Rokeach (1975), after making several criticisms of value clarification, said:

> All such reservations about values clarification notwithstanding, I believe that the values-clarification movement has made an extremely important contribution to modern education. It has succeeded in getting across the proposition that beyond making students aware of facts and concepts it is also important to make them aware of their own values. Such a broadening of educational objectives now has a universal face validity, largely because of the pioneering work of proponents of values clarification.

Personally, I do not think value clarification has *universal* validity, but I think the substance of Rokeach's comment is correct. Assuming this, where does value clarification go from here? Four possible directions present themselves:

1. *The "traditional" value-clarification approach will remain a distinct and viable force in education, in parenting, and in the helping professions for several years to come.* Over the last decade or more, certain names and principles have become associated with the value-clarification approach—Raths, Harmin, Simon, Kirschenbaum, Howe; valuing process, seven processes, seven criteria; Values Associates, National Humanistic Education Center, Humanistic Educators Network. Almost every publication on value clarification has referred to some of these constructs or groups or individuals as the basis for the author's work. Through their writings and workshops and organizational efforts, this group of individuals and their colleagues have coordinated and facilitated a growing interest in the value-clarification approach (as well as other approaches to humanizing education).

This group shows every sign of remaining viable for some time to come. Its members continue to offer workshops; to publish, sponsor, or facilitate research; to speak at many conferences and meetings; to co-ordinate a network of trainers; and to develop new applications for their work.

The importance of this lies in the fact that they have continued to work in the tradition of Raths' theory of value clarification. Thus, people who subscribe to value clarification can continue to identify with the theory, the strategies, the subject-matter orientation, and the research—all of which have a greater cumulative impact than any of the individuals involved. My prediction is that this tradition in value clarification will remain strong for several more years—developing new and better theory, research, materials, and methods and continuing to reach an increasingly larger number of both professionals and laypersons.

2. Simultaneously, almost paradoxically, *value clarification will take on a life of its own, apart from its traditional associations.* This fact is almost inevitable, and one that we have encouraged by choosing to "give the approach away" by publishing all the strategies in the *Handbook* and by not trying to control, franchise, or certify value-clarification trainers, or to establish "value clarification" as a registered trademark.

Thus, the term "value clarification" will appear more and more without credit, footnote, reference, or elaboration. I saw it yesterday in an article that listed value clarification among a series of other approaches: "role-playing, simulation, values clarification and group dynamics."

In this general sense, the term, I believe, will come to suggest an approach that (1) legitimizes a focus on controversial and personally important issues, and (2) allows students to think for themselves and make their own choices, without indoctrination or moralizing from the teacher or leader. This is fine and is certainly consistent with value clarification as traditionally described. But this general concept of value clarification may differ from traditional value clarification by failing to describe and teach any *systematic* valuing process. Bull sessions are fine when an interesting topic is suggested and everybody says what they think about it. But that is a relatively low level of value clarification. I predict that of all the new approaches, materials, and workshops that will use the rubric "value clarification," a great number will be little more than this type of warmed-over class discussion with interesting types of stimuli and activities to facilitate the discussion. That is good, as far as it goes; however, it will not be the kind of value clarification we have advocated for many years—grounded in theory and pointed toward systematic, even behavioral objectives for valuing proficiency.

Of course, along with the proliferation of the term, there will be materials and training that do not meet even these two minimal criteria for value clarification. We will see old texts reprinted with a pretty cover and the word "value" in the title and advertised as part of "a new value-clarification series." We will see moralizing disguised and called value clarification.

3. *Value clarification will be subjected to increasing criticism.* This is another concomitant of popularity. The academic community will call it "superficial," "value free," without sound theoretical or research base, and so on (issues discussed in Chapter 1). This criticism will do little to deter teachers from using it, although it might affect some administrators and funding sources.

An increasing amount of the criticism, however, will come from various parent and community groups. Some of this will be radical right wing criticism that will equate value clarification with communism, brainwashing, behavioral modification, and the like. Although value clarification is exactly the opposite of that, they will have difficulty believing it; because value clarification wants to have young people discuss controversial issues and reach their own conclusions, while this group knows there is only one correct set of conclusions for almost all controversial issues. Another group, with many parents and clergy, will oppose value clarification out of insecurity. Their authority over their children is diminishing, for many complex historical and social reasons. They will see value clarification as a further threat to that authority and influence. I can understand this. I would not want my child to be exposed, day in and day out, to an educational situation which I thought was harmful to his or her overall development. Some of these people, when they come to better understand value clarification, will change their minds. Others will continue to insist that the schools have no business dealing with certain value and moral issues that have traditionally been left to the home and the church.

This raises a complicated legal and political question that is not particular to value clarification. Who should exert what types of control over the schools? Parents, teachers' unions, students, school boards, administrators, state boards of education each make a case for some type of legitimate authority over the process of education. It will be many years before these questions of control will be settled. Until that time, programs such as value clarification will be caught in the middle of political crosscurrents and will try to survive as best they can.

Lest these predictions seem exaggerated, I should mention that in the last few years I have learned of several school districts in which value clarification was banned and several others in which it was under serious attack. I have seen several flyers distributed by such radical groups as the John Birch society that scurrilously attack value clarification, usually taking quotations, voting questions, or strategies out of context. And I recently saw a report describing how the *Values Clarification Handbook* was one of several books introduced in Congress as an example of the decadent immoral approaches being introduced in our schools. I have received copies of pending legislation in several states banning any form of humanistic education; discussion of values, attitudes, and other "controversial" issues; and student-to-student feedback.

While these challenges should be taken seriously, they should be seen in context. Most parents and clergy will continue to support or be indifferent to value clarification, and the constitutional protection of free speech will continue to apply to teachers and students. But the vocal minority will increasingly be heard from. Sometimes value clarification will be attacked by itself; other times it will be lumped with other approaches, which may or may not be similar (such as encounter groups). Sometimes it will be difficult or impossible to differentiate the irrational criticism from the thoughtful, concerned parents. But controversy will continue and increase, and those involved in value clarification and other approaches to humanistic education will have to begin thinking and planning strategies to better inform the public about their goals and methods.

4. *Value clarification will be expanded and integrated with other approaches.* Raths' seven valuing processes and the strategies and curriculum model that grew directly out of it were certainly pioneering work in the field of value education and humanistic education. But there are other conceptions of value and moral development, other sets of activities, and other curriculum models that also make significant contributions to value education and to the process of human growth and development. While there are advantages in isolating value clarification as a separate and distinct approach, there are also disadvantages. We could blind ourselves to new knowledge about human growth and development, to new educational approaches that have proven effective, to research from other schools that calls into question some of our own practices. To put it differently, if Louis Raths had been born in 1940 and had spent fifty years studying the process of value development, the theory he would have crystallized in 1990 would almost surely be quite different from that which he formulated during the forties and fifties. Why? Because he would have been informed by a half century of new knowledge.

Some theories last longer than others, but the history of ideas shows clearly how, one by one, older theories fall away, to be replaced by newer, more integrative theories, theories that encompass more data, that are more consistent with new and old knowledge, and that generate new discoveries and practices, both in science and in daily living. Value clarification will not last forever, nor should it. It is a step along the way.

REFERENCE

Rokeach, M. Toward a philosophy of value education. In J. Meyer, B. Burnham, & J. Cholvat (Eds.), *Values education: Theory, practice, problems, prospects*. Waterloo, Ontario: Wilfred Laurier University Press, 1975.

APPENDIX

VALUE CLARIFICATION: AN ANNOTATED BIBLIOGRAPHY, 1965-1975

In recent years, the amount of literature to emerge relating to values and education has been immense. The task of reviewing and reporting this wealth of written material is further magnified when related fields, such as anthropology, guidance and counseling, philosophy, psychology, religion, and sociology are examined.

In his doctoral dissertation, Superka (1973) noted, *"Educational Index* (1929–1971) lists over 900 articles on values, more than two-thirds of which have been written since 1960" (p. 12). He stated further:

> An examination of the indices of the *Dissertation Abstracts International* dramatically demonstrates the recent upsurge of research interest in values. The cumulative index (ranging from the 1940s to 1969) catalogues approximately 80 dissertations on values, the vast majority in the last decade of that period. The indices from 1970 to 1973 list an average of 13 references each month—over 150 dissertations on values during each of those years. (p. 12)

Additionally, there have been three comprehensive bibliographies on values. In 1959, Albert and Kluckhohn compiled *A Selected Bibliography on Values, Ethics, and Esthetics in the Behavioral Sciences and Philosophy, 1920–1958*, which included almost 200 references. Raths, Harmin, and Simon's 1966 book, *Values and Teaching*, listed approximately 100 sources that contributed to the formulation of their value-clarification theory. Thomas published *A Comprehensive Bibliography*

The original version of this bibliography, compiled by H. Kirschenbaum, B. Glaser-Kirschenbaum, and R. D. Gray, III, was published by the National Humanistic Education Center, 1976. Used with permission.

on the Value Concept (1967) that contained nearly 800 articles and books on values, most of which were written in the last thirty years.

A Value-Clarification Bibliography

The bibliography that follows is much more specialized in focus than any of those cited above. This annotated bibliography is an outgrowth of Raths, Harmin, and Simon's book *Values and Teaching* (1966). Because of the interest and productivity that book sparked, the theory of value clarification has grown and developed in both diversity and complexity. Thus, this bibliography is devoted entirely to the sources that can be directly related to the value-clarification theory, process, and practice. Criteria for inclusion were as follows:

1. The item was published in 1965 or later (that is, during or after the publication of the book *Values and Teaching*).

2. The author(s) gave a prominent position to one or more of the following in the publication:

   (a) Raths' seven criteria or processes of valuing
   (b) A reference to original writings or key individuals in the value-clarification movement
   (c) The concepts, language and/or methods of value clarification

3. The publication was *not* primarily a research study. This criterion was included to avoid repeating Kirschenbaum's (1975) "Current Research in Values Clarification" (#172), which describes about twenty empirical studies completed in the past decade.

Clearly, applying these criteria eliminated many excellent writings on the subject of values, including scores of articles and books that may be entirely consistent with the goals and methods of value clarification.

There were several motivating factors that prompted the publication of this bibliography: (1) we felt it was important to chronicle the significant number of value-clarification writings that have been published in the last several years; (2) we wanted to show that the value-clarification movement has not been the product of a limited few, but rather the individual and combined efforts of many people in numerous fields of interest; and (3) most important, we hoped that other individuals, by gaining perspective on what has already been developed in value clarification, would see new directions for carrying the work further—applying value clarification in new fields, modifying older value-clarification theory and practices, and applying the rigors of research to the value-clarification approach.

One final word is necessary. We may have omitted some items that should have been included in this bibliography. The most likely reason for this omission was our lack of knowledge that they existed or our inability to obtain copies of them for annotation. We would welcome, therefore, copies of any articles, publications, or materials that should be included in a revised version of this bibliography. These items should be sent to the authors in care of the National Humanistic Education Center, 110 Spring Street, Saratoga Springs, N.Y. 12866.

References

Albert, E. M., & Kluckhohn, C. *Selected bibliography on values, ethics, and esthetics in the behavioral sciences and philosophy: 1920–1958*. New York: Free Press, 1959.

Superka, D. *A typology of valuing theories and values education approaches.* Unpublished doctoral dissertation, University of California, Berkeley, Calif., 1973.

Thomas, W. *A comprehensive bibliography on the values concept.* Grand Rapids, Mich.: Project on Student Values, 1967.

THE BIBLIOGRAPHY

1965

1. Harmin, M., & Simon, S. B. The subject matter controversy revisited. *Peabody Journal of Education*, 1965, *42*(4), 194–205.

   This article introduces the three levels of subject matter—fact, generalization, and value-oriented levels—and applies them to the Pilgrim story, the Shakespearean play *Macbeth* and Newton's Laws of Motion. It suggests that schools move from a focus on facts to a greater emphasis on the second and third levels as a means of making learning more exciting and meaningful.

2. Lieberman, P., & Simon, S. B. Values and student writing. *Educational Leadership*, 1965, *22*(6), 414–421; 438.

   This is the fullest discussion of the Value Card strategy in the value-clarification literature. It includes many examples of students' value cards, an extended rationale for their use, many variations on the basic strategy, and many helpful suggestions for the teacher.

3. Lieberman, P., & Simon, S. B. Current events and values. *Social Education*, 1965, *29*(8), 523–533.

   Advocating that value-clarification strategies be an integral part of current events curricula, the writers provide examples of Value Sheets with controversial statements followed by clarifying questions. Value Sheets included are: (a) a quote from Pastor Niemoller titled "Speak Up"; (b) an article by C. A. Walls titled "The Price of Peace"; and (c) an excerpt from *Core-later* titled "Long Island Pickets."

1966

4. Harmin, M. Values in the classroom: An alternative to moralizing. In W. Rogge and G. E. Stormer (Eds.), *Inservice training for teachers of the gifted.* Champaign, Ill.: Stipes Publishing, 1966.

   A variety of strategies are presented to provide teachers with classroom methods for helping children develop their own values. Examples include Value Sheets dealing with the areas of financial priorities and public affirmation of beliefs, the Devil's Advocate strategy exploring the topic of space travel, a Thought Sheet, and several Continua.

5. Raths, L., Harmin, M., & Simon, S. B. *Values and Teaching.* Columbus, Ohio: Charles E. Merrill, 1966.

   This is the first major book on value clarification. Initially, a theoretical section is presented with chapters on "The Difficulty of Developing Values," "Values and Valuing," and "Teaching for Value Clarity." The second part has chapters on the Clarifying Response, Value Sheets, and a brief discussion of eighteen other strategies. The third section focuses on applying the value theory with chapters titled: "Getting Started, Guidelines and Problems"; "Emotional Needs, Thinking and Valuing"; and "Research Completed and Needed."

1967

6. Harmin, M., & Simon, S. B. Values and teaching: A humane process. *Educational Leadership*, 1967, *24*(6), 517–525.

   Examples of several strategies included are Clarifying Questions, Value Sheets on the issues of financial priorities and public affirmation of beliefs, Values Continua on the topics of personal freedom, seat belts and military service, and Thought Sheets.

7. Harmin, M., & Simon, S. B. Working with values in the classroom. *Scholastic Teacher*, 1967, *89*(13), 16–17; 24.

   An introduction to value-clarification is provided for classroom teachers along with examples of the following: Value Sheets, Continua, the Devil's Advocate, and Zig-Zag strategy.

8. Raths, L., Harmin, M., & Simon, S. B. Helping children clarify values. *Today's Education*, 1967, *56*(7), 12–15.

   In light of rapid social change and the varying desirability of particular values, the authors offer teachers the "seven valuing processes" as an alternative to traditional methods of teaching values. A detailed description and explanation of the Clarifying Response is provided, followed by a brief presentation of the Value Sheet strategy.

1968

9. Clegg, A. A., Jr., & Hills, J. L. A strategy for exploring values and valuing in the social studies. *The College of Education Record*, University of Washington, May 1968, 67–68.

Contending that the schools constitute a major influence in shaping children's values, the authors urge teachers to adopt instructional materials designed to help students explore value issues. They present an instructional model in which they integrate Taba's approach to cognitive tasks with Raths' valuing processes. A pilot study is described in which this teaching strategy is applied to a fifth-grade social studies curriculum.

10. Hafeman, J. Teaching and valuing process. *Wisconsin Education Association*, 1968, *100*(10), 5.

This editorial comment supports the need for schools and educators to teach a process of valuing modeled after the work of Raths, Harmin, and Simon. The author feels this is a major way for teachers to combine the affective domain with the cognitive to help students develop their maximum potential, determine their own values and become more effective citizens in a democratic society.

11. Harmin, M. & Simon, S. B. Using the humanities for value clarification. *Impact*, Spring 1968, *8*(3), 27–30.

In addition to teaching the factual and conceptual levels of humanities subject matter, teachers can emphasize the values level. Examples of these three levels of teaching are provided for the American Pilgrim story and Shakespeare's *Macbeth*.

12. Klevan, A. Clarifying as a teaching process. *Educational Leadership*, 1968, *25*(5), 454–455; 457–458.

The author provides a list of clarifying responses a teacher might make to a student who has expressed a value or thoughtful opinion. For greater emphasis, these clarifying procedures have been grouped into two modes: reflective and dissonant responses. Two major characteristics of clarifying questions are noted.

1969

13. Harmin, M., Kirschenbaum, H., & Simon, S. B. Teaching history with a focus on values. *Social Education*, 1969, *33*(5), 568–570.

Using the three-level concept of subject matter (facts, concepts, and values), the authors show how lessons on the U.S. Constitution and the topic of "war" might be taught with a focus on the students' values.

14. Harmin, M., Nisenholtz, B., & Simon, S. B. Teaching for value clarity. *Changing Education*, Spring 1969, *4*(1), 20–22.

A consideration is made of the values confusion and struggle of urban slum children. The disparity between children's desires and the social and economic realities that must be confronted is noted. The authors urge that educators teach the valuing process as a means of helping students sort out many of the conflicting issues and desires with which they must deal. A variety of action-oriented projects are surveyed as a means of assisting students to act upon their values and to perceive themselves as capable of effecting changes in their lives.

15. Kirschenbaum, H., & Simon, S. B. Teaching English with a focus on values. *The English Journal*, 1969, *58*(7), 1071–1076; 1113.

The Value Sheet strategy can be used effectively in the English classroom. Examples are given showing how teachers can use the Value Sheet to help teach literature, poetry, composition, and discussion in a more meaningful way by focusing on values.

16. Raths, L. E. *Teaching for learning*. Columbus, Ohio: Charles E. Merrill, 1969.

Raths, who originally developed the value-clarification theory, describes ten major components of teaching. One of these components deals directly with value clarification and education. Raths feels that a teacher should guide the student's value development especially in his or her experiences with other students, and offer the opportunity to clarify value issues. The use of clarifying questions is discussed and illustrated.

17. Simon, S. B. Promoting the search for values. *Education Opportunity Forum*, Fall 1969, *1*(4), 75–84.

Following a brief introduction describing the need for value clarification, the author presents several strategies designed to help students develop their own values. Included are Weekly Reaction Sheets, Weekly Value Cards, an Autobiographical Questionnaire, Time Diary, Confrontation Questioning, Value Sheets, and a description of a values-confrontation experience.

18. Simon, S. B., & Carnes, A. Teaching Afro-American history with a focus on values. *Educational Leadership*, 1969, *27*(3), 222–224.

After a brief discussion of the need for value clarification, the following strategies are discussed in connection with Afro-American history: Rank Ordering, Value Continuum, Devil's Advocate Open-Minded Question, Role Playing, and the Value Sheet.

19. Simon, S. B., & Harmin, M. Subject matter with a focus on values. *Educational Leadership*, 1969, *26*(1), 34–39. Reprinted as Focus on values for more relevant schools. *New Jersey Education Association Review*, 1969, *43*(2).

The authors present the three-levels theory of subject matter (fact, concept, value) with examples from the U.S. Constitution and Shakespeare's *Hamlet*.

1970

20. Cheney, R. Youth, sexuality and values clarification. *Findings*, Fall 1970, 14–16.

   Specific reference is made to the conflicting values and standards young people face in the area of human sexuality. In addition to describing the theory of value clarification and listing some useful resources, the article relates the experiences of using the value-clarifying process with a group of high school students during a summer religious retreat. This process helped the young people make decisions about their relationships with members of the opposite sex.

21. Harmin, M., Kirschenbaum, H. & Simon, S. B. The search for values with a focus on math. *Teaching mathematics in the elementary school*. Washington, D.C.: National Association of Elementary School Principals, National Educators Assocation and the National Council of Teachers of Mathematics, 1970.

   The authors show how teaching mathematics and value clarification fit together. They provide numerous examples of how math problems, projects, and assignments can be taught with a focus on values.

22. Harmin, M., Kirschenbaum, H., & Simon, S. B. Teaching science with a focus on values. *Science Teacher*, 1970, *37*(1), 16–20.

   The authors argue that teaching science can and should help students clarify their own values and the values implied within the content and instructional process. Using the three-levels concept of subject matter (fact, concept, and value), they provide numerous examples of value-level teaching with units on Newton's Laws of Motion, the earth's crust, electricity, weather, dissecting a frog, and a dozen other science topics.

23. Kirschenbaum, H. The listening game. *Colloquy*, 1970, *3*(8), 12–15.

   Reflections on a conversation between two women, overheard on a train, lead to thoughts on inter-generation communication and how to help young people make their own decisions. Two strategies for better communication and decision making are then described—Rogerian Listening and the Free Choice Game.

24. Kirschenbaum, H. Sensitivity modules. *Media and Methods*, 1970, *6*(6), 36–38.

   A discussion of the sensitivity module strategy is presented including its purposes and risks. Examples of sensitivity modules on the themes of race and poverty are given. Additionally, examples of modules for use with young children and subject matter are listed.

25. Michalak, D. A. The clarification of values. *Improving College and University Teaching*, Spring 1970, *18*(2), 100–101.

   The author discusses how curriculum reshuffling does not substantially assist students in dealing with such basic issues as human and societal relationships. He advocates the use of strategies for clarifying values. The article stresses that values are not clarified in learning environments where imitation, imposition, or rote memorization occur. Clarification occurs when teacher and student engage in reflective thinking and question the "whys" behind values.

26. Rees, F. D. Teaching values through health education. *School Health Review*, 1970, *1*(1), 15–17.

    The author describes the value clarification process in health education as a meaningful way of helping students to construct their own set of values. In addition, he touches on other related issues, such as establishing a psychologically permissive learning environment, identifying health curriculum areas in which values teaching can occur, and instituting value education in teacher preparation programs.

27. Schindler-Rainman, E. Are values out of style? *Journal of the National Association of Women Deans and Counselors*, Fall 1970, 18–22.

    A description is offered identifying three ways of examining values, three types of value dilemmas, three stances for value educators, a value dilemma exercise, and a section on the characteristics of a value educator.

28. Shattuck, J. B. Using the sciences for value clarification. *Science Education*, 1970, *54*(1), 9–11.

    Instead of a conventional approach that emphasizes only factual and conceptual levels, Shattuck advocates the addition of a third level—a value, or "you" level. The author provides examples of how science questions and information can be presented at the factual, conceptual, and value levels.

29. Simon, S. B. Sensitizing modules: A cure for "senioritis." *Scholastic Teacher*, September 21, 1970, 28–29; 42.

    In an effort to vitalize twelfth-grade curricula and assuage senior restlessness, the author proposes a variety of experiential activities designed to increase students' social awareness and confront them with real value issues and concerns. Examples of twenty-five sensitivity modules on issues of race and poverty are described.

30. Simon, S. B. Three ways to teach church school. *Colloquy*, 1970, *3*(1), 37–38.

    The three levels of teaching are discussed and examples are taken from the story of Jesus' triumphant entrance into Jerusalem and the life of Saint Francis of Assisi.

31. Simon, S. B. Your values are showing. *Colloquy*, 1970, *3*(1), 20–32.

This article provides descriptions and examples of numerous value-clarification strategies, including (a) Value Sheets on the topics of football, migrant harvesters, and international peace, (b) Weekly Value Cards, (c) Value Continua on the military and on racial conflict, (d) Confrontation Questions using the Who Comes to Your House strategy, (e) Rank Orders of famous civil leaders and ways to eliminate slums, (f) Time Diary, (g) Autobiographical Questionnaire, (h) Weekly Reaction Sheets, (i) List of Sensitivity Modules, and (j) Action Projects.

32. Simon, S. B., & Wright, H. *Values systems techniques*. Film. New York: Episcopal Church, 1970.

A twenty-eight minute, 16mm. black and white film, showing Dr. Simon leading a panel of senior high school students in a demonstration of four value-clarification strategies: Values Voting, Rank Ordering, Proud Whip, and Public Interview. The film may be rented at a minimal fee from ROA's Films, 1969 North Astor Street, Milwaukee, Wis.

33. Westerhoff, J. H., III. How can we teach values? *Colloquy*, 1970, *3*(1), 17–19.

The editor of *Colloquy* reviews Raths, Harmin, and Simon's book *Values and Teaching*. He uses this review to discuss the need for value clarification and for teaching the valuing process. He concludes by applying the valuing approach to religious education.

1971

34. Harmin, M., & Simon, S. B. Values. In D. Allen and E. Seifman (Eds.), *Teachers handbook*. Glenview, Ill.: Scott, Foresman, 1971.

Three major alternatives for dealing with values are examined: (a) to do nothing about values; (b) to "transmit" values using various approaches, such as modeling, rewards and punishment, manipulation, etc.; and (c) to "clarify values" using the "clarifying liberal arts approach" and the "value skills approach." Critical consideration is given to the issues and implications presented by each of these alternatives. A bibliography on value approaches is included.

35. Kirschenbaum, H. *Clarifying values at the family table*. Upper Jay, New York: Adirondack Mountain Humanistic Education Center, 1971.

This occasional paper presents a description and rationale for the Family Circle strategy, a variation of the Value Whip strategy. Fifty-two Family Circle topics are given with special examples on circle topics for holidays, vacations, and guests.

36. Kirschenbaum, H. *Teaching home economics with a focus on values*. Upper Jay, New York: Adirondack Mountain Humanistic Education Center, 1971.

Using examples created and used by home economics teachers for their classrooms, this occasional paper shows how five value-clarification strategies can be used with home economics students and issues. The strategies are Unfinished Sentences, Sensitivity Modules, Rank Orders, Proud Lines, and Chairs or Dialogue with Self.

37. Kirschenbaum, H. & Bacher, R. *Clarifying our values: A listening post program.* Minneapolis, Minn.: Augsburg Publishing House, 1971.

Detailed instructions are presented for conducting a ninety-minute value-clarification session with high-school-age students. Strategies included are Strongly Agree/Strongly Disagree, the Values Grid, Rank Orders, and Proud Line.

38. Simon, S. B. Dinner table learning. *Colloquy,* 1971, *4*(11), 34–37.

To help make the evening meal an interesting and provocative learning experience, a variety of value strategies are presented with guidelines for their use. Examples included are the Coat of Arms, Rank Orders, Twenty Things I Love To Do, Family Circle topics, and Value Sheets.

39. Simon, S. B. The search for values. *Edvance,* 1971, *1*(3), 1–3; 6.

Not available for annotation.

40. Simon, S. B. Two newer strategies for value clarification. *Edvance,* 1971, *2*(1), 6.

Two value-clarification strategies (Twenty Things I Love To Do and "I Learned" Statements) are described.

41. Simon, S. B. Values clarification vs. indoctrination. *Social Education,* 1971, *35*(8), 902–905; 915.

The value-clarification approach to values education is offered as an alternative to indoctrination, moralizing, or the denial of value issues. Five strategies are described: Twenty Things I Love To Do, "I Learned" Statements, Baker's Dozen, "I Urge" Telegrams, and Personal Coat of Arms.

42. Simon, S. B., Daitch, P., & Hartwell, M. Value clarification: New mission for religious education. *Catechist,* 1971, *5*(1), 8–9; 31.

This is the first of three articles designed for religious educators who wish to help children develop a sense of worth and identity and increase their ability to make choices and confront moral dilemmas. Strategies presented include Clarifying Questions, Twenty Things I Love To Do, "I Learned" Statements, High Point Identification, and Value Cards.

43. Simon, S. B., Daitch, P., & Hartwell, M. Value clarification: Part II. *Catechist,* 1971, *5*(2), 36–38.

A second article for religious educators who wish to assist children in developing the valuing process. The value theory is presented and the following strategies are introduced: The Value Grid, Coat of Arms, Alligator River, and Hair Biography.

44. Simon, S. B., Daitch, P., & Hartwell, M. Value clarification: Part III. *Catechist*, 1971, *5*(3), 28–29.

In the final article of a series that introduces value clarification to religious educators, the authors present Jesus as one who had a clear set of values that He publicly affirmed and acted upon consistently. Similarly, they urge teachers to serve as models of the Christian life. Contending that the presence of beliefs is necessary for the valuing criteria of affirmation and action to be met, they offer four more strategies designed to help students examine their beliefs. The strategies include Time Diary, Fallout Shelter, "I Urge" Telegrams, and People Like Me.

45. Simon, S. B., & Sparago, E. Values: Clarification and action. *Momentum*, 1971, *2*(4), 4–9.

A religious-existential discussion asserting the importance of self-exploration and the determination of one's own values opens the article. This is followed by two examples of three-levels teaching describing Jesus' triumphant entry into Jerusalem and the life of Saint Francis of Assisi. Additionally, five value-clarification strategies are presented: Twenty Things I Love To Do, Value Statements, Confrontation Questioning, Value Continua, and Rank Orders. The article concludes with Simon sharing how he acts on some of his own values and the consequences of these actions.

46. *Workshop on values clarification*. New York: Seabury Press. (Complete reference not available.)

A design for a ten-hour value-clarification workshop.

1972

47. Abramowitz, M., & Macari, C. Values clarification in junior high school. *Educational Leadership*, 1972, *29*(7), 621–626.

Two school administrators discuss the need for value clarification in a Black and Puerto Rican high school. Examples of five strategies are provided: Twenty Things I Love To Do, Alternatives Search, Value Voting, Continuum, and Rank Orders.

48. Curwin, G. Pages from my autobiography. *Trend*, Spring 1972, *8*(1).

Not available for annotation.

49. Curwin, G., Curwin, R., Kramer, R. M., Simon, M. J., & Walsh, K. *Search for values*. Villa Maria, Pa.: The Center for Learning, 1972.

This collection of seven structured units is designed to assist junior and senior high school students in personally exploring their values on the topics of (a) time, (b) competition, (c) authority, (d) personal space, (e) commitment, (f) relationships, and (g) images. The package consists of an instructor's manual and seven envelopes (one for each unit) containing a total of seventy-seven duplicator masters of various strategy sheets.

50. Gellatt, H. B., Varenhorst, B., & Carey, R. *Deciding: A leader's guide* and *Deciding: A student workbook*. New York: College Entrance Examination Board, 1972.

    The authors design a decision-making unit for high school students using much of the value-clarification theory as background and several value-clarification exercises including Twenty Things I Love To Do, "I Learned" Statements, Coat of Arms, Proud Whip, plus many of their own. Three sections of the guide correspond to what the authors say students need for effective decision making, namely, values, information, and strategy.

51. Goodman, J. An application of value clarification to the teaching of psychology. *Periodically* (American Psychological Association), 1972, *2*(4).

    The Fall-Out Shelter Problem strategy is presented with several suggested follow-up activities that make the exercise useful in teaching concepts and theories in social psychology.

52. Goodman, J., & Hawkins, L. Value clarification: Meeting a challenge in education. *Colloquy*, 1972, *5*(5), 15–18.

    A detailed description of the first session of an eight week value-clarification course offered by two graduate students to a group of undergraduates in a college dormitory. The following strategies are described: Name Tags, Here-and-Now Wheel, Alligator River, Pattern Search, Dear Me Letters, and brief descriptions of several others.

53. Gray, F. Doing something about values. *Learning*, 1972, *1*(2), 15–18.

    The author describes his experiences in a two-day value-clarification workshop conducted by Sidney B. Simon. Mixed in with this description are the author's observations of value clarification as it is used in several schools. Included are excerpts of an interview with Dr. Simon.

54. Gray, F., Kohlberg and Simon. *Learning*, 1972, *1*(2), 19.

    In this brief exchange of opinions, Kohlberg and Simon talk with *Learning* magazine about their respective ideas and how they are related.

55. Hawley, R. C. Values and decision making. *Independent School Bulletin*, 1972, *32*(1), 19–23.

    The author discusses the need for value clarification, reviews Raths' seven valuing processes, and describes the open-accept-stimulate sequence of value clarification in a classroom. He gives examples of the following seven strategies: Value Voting, Rank Ordering, Forced Choice Games—including the Fall-Out Shelter Problem and Alligator River, Value Whips, Value Cards, "I Learned" Statements, and the Here-and-Now Wheel.

56. Howe, L. Group dynamics and values clarification. *Penney's Forum*, Spring/Summer 1972, 12.

This article examines several student seating arrangements, considers the group dynamics facilitated by each seating arrangement, and discusses how these group dynamics would affect the use of value-clarification strategies.

57. Kelly, P., & Conroy, G. A promotive health plan preventing alcohol and drug abuse in the schools. *Arizona Medicine*, January 1972.

The authors state that drug abuse is merely a symptom that must be cured by building a healthy psychological foundation. This foundation consists of a positive self-concept—the "IALAC" concept is described—and an effective "valuing process."

58. Kirschenbaum, H. *The free choice English curriculum*. Upper Jay, N. Y.: Adirondack Mountain Humanistic Education Center, 1972.

This occasional paper shows how a junior or senior high school English department can help students develop both their own values and a better appreciation of literature and writing. In the "free choice" curriculum, students choose their English course from a variety of English department offerings. Many examples are provided and the realities of such a change are discussed.

59. Knapp, C. E. Attitudes and values in environmental education. *The Journal of Environmental Education*, Summer 1972, *3*(4), 26–29.

This paper briefly defines "attitudes" and "values," discusses the role of teachers and schools in teaching attitudes and values, and examines some of the research in the area of environmental attitudes.

60. Knapp, C. E. The environment: Children explore their values. *Instructor Magazine*, 1972, *81*(7), 116–118.

A discussion of the need for value clarification in environmental education and a presentation of strategies to help students explore their environmental values. This article was later expanded into "Teaching Environmental Education with a Focus on Values," #61 in this bibliography.

61. Knapp, C. E. *Teaching environmental education with a focus on values*. Upper Jay, N.Y.: Adirondack Mountain Humanistic Edu-

cation Center, 1972.

After discussing how the seven valuing processes relate to environmental education, the author presents examples of how to use the valuing strategies in connection with the subject. Strategies presented include the following: Value Sheets, Pictures Without Captions, Role Playing, Continuum, Open-Ended Sentences, Time Diaries, Autobiographical Questionnaire, Voting Questions, Rank Orders, and other class activities.

62. Proudman, C. *Values*. New York: Friendship Press, 1972.

A board game for three to six players. Depending on where the spin wheel stops, players choose a card from several piles. Each card contains a value topic or problem. Depending on game variables, the player may do one of the following: (a) answer one question from the other players on the selected topic, (b) make a statement on the topic, or (c) choose to be interviewed on one of the related areas of conflict and confusion.

63. Rees, F. D. Teaching the valuing process in sex education. *School Health Review*, 1972, *3*(2), 2–4.

The need for education about human sexuality is expressed. The article describes various approaches that educators have employed, emphasizes the need for young people to formulate their own values regarding sexuality, outlines a five-step valuing process, and includes classroom activities to implement the process.

64. Simon, S. B. Election year and dinner table learning. *Colloquy*, 1972, *5*(9), 23–25.

Focusing on election year topics, the article describes several value-clarification strategies for use with children during the evening meal. The following examples are included: Value Voting topics, Rank Orders, Designing Buttons, "I Urge" Telegrams, Pictures Without Captions, "If" Situations, Where Do You Draw the Line?, and Value Sheets.

65. Simon, S. B. The teacher educator in value development. *Phi Delta Kappan*, 1972, *53*(10), 649–651.

An introduction and summary argue the need for value clarification as a part of teacher training. The bulk of the article describes six strategies for accomplishing this purpose: Twenty Things I Love To Do, "I Learned that . . ." Statements, Coat of Arms, Bakers Dozen, Opposite Quadrants, and the Value Sheet titled "We're Really Getting It Together, Man."

66. Simon, S. B. Values clarification and shalom. *Colloquy*, 1972, *5*(7), 18–21.

The concept of "shalom" is examined through the use of eight value-clarification strategies: What You Know and What You Don't Know, Unfinished Sentences, Priority Ladder—Forced Choice Ladder, Rank Ordering, Significant Others in Your Life, Where Do You Draw the Line?, and the Value Sheet titled "Composition For Personal Growth."

67. Simon, S. B. What do you value? *Penney's Forum*, Spring/ Summer 1972, 4–5.

    Instructions for the use of the following three value-clarification strategies: Twenty Things I Love To Do, Coat of Arms, and Baker's Dozen.

68. Simon, S. B., Curwin, G., & Hartwell, M. Teaching values. *Girl Scout Leader*, 1972, *14*(4), 12–13.

    After an introduction to value clarification, the authors present various value strategies focusing on Girl-Scout-related interests and materials. Exercises include using Girl Scout song lyrics as a Value Sheet, an inventory of "helping times," Unfinished Sentences, a strategy for sharing "positive points," and five "Fantasy Seeds."

69. Simon, S. B., & Hartwell, M. Personal growth through advertising. *Colloquy*, 1972, *5*(11), 12–15.

    The argument is presented that teachers have a responsibility for helping their students negotiate the impact advertising has on their lives. It stresses that students who have learned the skills of critically examining advertisements, coupled with the skills of self-exploration, can significantly raise their awareness levels and make more valid choices. The authors provide eight exercises to assist teachers in developing a unit on personal growth through advertising.

70. Simon, S. B., Howe, L. & Kirschenbaum, H. *Values clarification: A handbook of practical strategies for teachers and students*. New York: Hart, 1972.

    The second major work on value clarification pulls together much of the developmental work completed since the publication of *Values and Teaching*. After an overview of the value-clarification approach and a chapter on the use of the handbook, the remainder of the book is devoted to describing seventy-nine value-clarification strategies. Included with each strategy is a section for purpose, procedures, examples, variations, and notes to the teacher. Hundreds of examples are provided for such basic strategies as Voting, Rank Ordering, and so on. Additionally, examples are grouped appropriately for different age levels.

71. Simon, S. B., Kirschenbaum, H., & Fuhrmann, B. *An introduction to values clarification*. New York: J. C. Penney Company, 1972.

    A packaged seven-session teaching unit that is specially designed for teachers. For each session, there is a folder containing instructions to the teacher, as well as wall charts, overhead transparencies, value sheets, etc. All seven folders with introductions are contained in a box. The whole kit may be rented, at no cost, from the Consumer Relations Department of any J. C. Penney store.

72. Simon, S. B., Kirschenbaum, H., & Howe, L. Strategies for value
    clarification. *Penney's Forum*, Spring/Summer 1972, 8–11.

    After an introduction to the seven valuing processes and the guidelines
    for using value-clarification exercises, the following three strategies are
    presented: What's in Your Wallet?, Unfinished Sentences, and Chairs or
    Dialogue with Self.

1973

73. Behling, H. E., Jr. What do we value in teacher education? *The
    Informer*, 1973, *3*(1), 1; 3.

    A discussion outlining the need for educators to become more aware of
    themselves and the values that guide and influence their lives and ac-
    tivities. The author notes the present lack of emphasis schools and col-
    leges place on value clarification and the valuing process. He concludes
    with a description of research findings by Carl Rogers in the area of
    positive teacher behavior changes after exposure to a program akin to
    value clarification.

74. Berson, M. B. Valuing, helping, thinking, resolving. *Childhood
    Education*, 1973, *49*(5), 242–245.

    A tribute is paid to Louis E. Raths, "father" of value clarification. It
    briefly reviews his life and major work, including his several books on
    values, emotional needs, and thinking.

75. Betof, E., & Kirschenbaum, H. *Teaching health education with a
    focus on values*. Upper Jay, N.Y.: National Humanistic Education
    Center, 1973.

    After briefly describing the need for value clarification in health educa-
    tion, the authors show how the topics of venereal disease and physical
    fitness could be taught on the fact, concept, and value levels. On the
    value level, they use Clarifying Questions, Rank Orders, Sentence Com-
    pletions, Continua, an Autobiographical Questionnaire, and Pictures
    Without Captions.

76. Frick, R. Values: Games are not enough. *Teacher*, 1973, *91*(4),
    8–9.

    After criticizing value-education approaches that utilize only superficial
    games, the author advocates teaching a valuing process that emphasizes
    studying alternatives and consequences. It is never clearly stated
    whether he places value clarification in the former or latter category.

77. Goodman, J. Sid Simon on values: No moralizers or manipulators
    allowed. *Nation's Schools*, 1973, *92*(6), 39–42.

    This interview with Sidney Simon presents an overview of the value-
    clarification theory, which Simon defines as a system for teaching the
    process of valuing. References are made to (a) Louis Raths' initial efforts

to develop the theory, (b) the use of strategies as the major vehicle for classroom implementation, (c) how students benefit from value clarification, and (d) future directions. Of special interest is Simon's explanation of the differences between how values are deposed, imposed, and exposed in classrooms.

78. Goodman, J., Simon, S., & Witort, R. Tackling racism by clarifying values. *Today's Education*, January 1973, *63*(1), 37–38.

Initially, the article argues for dealing with racism on the fact, concept, and value levels. The second part includes a story involving black-white conflict in a high school and presents a value-clarification exercise in which participants rank order characters in a story involving racism. Other ways to relate the story to personal values are included.

79. Green, D., Stewart, P., & Kirschenbaum, H. *Training a large public school system in values clarification*. Upper Jay, N.Y.: National Humanistic Education Center, 1973.

This occasional paper describes the story of how Harmin, Kirschenbaum, and Simon worked for four years with the Akron, Ohio, public schools, providing an intensive in-service education program for 450 teachers and training a team of Akron value specialists. The accomplishments and limitations of the training program are described.

80. Hall, B. *Values clarification as learning process: A sourcebook*. New York: Paulist Press, 1973.

A presentation of ideas and activities designed to be used by adults and, more specifically, by teachers and teacher-education programs. Its humanistic approach explores the issues of human values, life, and the search for meaning. Value-clarification theory and processes form the underlying structure for this sourcebook.

81. Hall, B. *Values clarification as learning process: A guidebook*. New York: Paulist Press, 1973.

This manual of projects and exercises is designed to help participants examine and clarify their values. Included are definitions of values and value indicators, classroom value techniques, and designs for value-clarification conferences.

82. Hall, B., & Smith, M. *Values clarification as learning process: Handbook for Christian educators*. New York: Paulist Press, 1973.

An exploration is made of valuing, of the theological bases of the value-clarification methodology, and of the applications valuing has for religious education, parish renewal, liturgy, and personal prayers.

83. Harmin, M. *People projects*. Menlo Park, Calif.: Addison-Wesley, 1973.

One hundred and twenty activities for elementary students are presented. Each project or task is printed on a large, illustrated laminated card, suitable for individual work or whole-class lessons. The materials deal with feelings, imagination, values, projects, and thinking that can be used in a self-directed program, learning center, or open classroom.

84. Harmin, M. *Making sense of our lives.* Niles, Ill.: Argus Communications, 1973–1974.

    A series of four value-rich topics are presented. The material for each topic includes a value sheet, motivational poster, and a teacher suggestion guide or lesson plan. These value sheets are suitable for entire class lessons or for independent and small-group study. Student directions are printed on each sheet. Each value sheet is available in spirit master form or on printed, bound pads. Activities can be purchased singly or in groups.

85. Harmin, M., Kirschenbaum, H., & Simon, S. B. *Clarifying values through subject matter: Applications for the classroom.* Minneapolis, Minn.: Winston Press, 1973.

    This work draws together and extends all the previous efforts the authors and their colleagues have done in combining value clarification with the teaching of subject matter. The three-levels concept of subject matter receives its fullest discussion to date. Examples of three-levels teaching are provided for every subject in the school curriculum. Other approaches to teaching subject matter with a focus on values are suggested.

86. Howe, L., Wolfe, D., Howe, M. M., & Keating, M. Clarifying values through foreign language study. *Hispania*, 1973, *56*(2), 404–406.

    A description of how to use the Voting, Ranking, and Continuum strategies in foreign language classes.

87. Hoy, T. *A values clarification design as an organizational development intervention.* Washington, D.C.: Project Test Pattern, 1973.

    A sophisticated use of the Value Continuum to help a group explore differences in perceptions, expectations, and values. The examples provided include church groups and a hospital staff, but the process could be used with any group or organization.

88. Kirschenbaum, H. Beyond values clarification. In H. Kirschenbaum & S. B. Simon (Eds.), *Readings in values clarification.* Minneapolis, Minn.: Winston Press, 1973.

    The author makes several criticisms of Raths' seven criteria for a value, argues for elimination of "criteria" in favor of "processes of valuing," relates the process of valuing to other process goals of humanistic education, and advocates the integration of various humanistic approaches using a new concept of "life processes" or "life skills."

89. Kirschenbaum, H. Values clarification in an organizational setting. In H. Kirschenbaum & S. B. Simon (Eds.), *Readings in values clarification*. Minneapolis, Minn.: Winston Press, 1973.

   In a planning letter to his colleague Merrill Harmin, Kirschenbaum describes a complete developmental sequence that will help a national organization develop an action program to clarify its values, goals, and future directions.

90. Kirschenbaum, H., & Glaser, B. *An annotated bibliography on values clarification*. Upper Jay, N.Y.: National Humanistic Education Center, 1973. An abridged version appears in H. Kirschenbaum and S. B. Simon (Eds.), *Readings in values clarification*. Minneapolis, Minn.: Winston Press, 1973.

   Following an introduction explaining their criteria for selection, the annotators cite and summarize seventy-five books and articles on value clarification that appeared between 1965 and February 1973.

91. Kirschenbaum, H., & Simon, S. B., (Eds.). *Readings in values clarification*. Minneapolis, Minn.: Winston Press, 1973.

   Major selections are titled Value Clarification and Other Perspectives, Value Clarification and School Subjects, Values in Religious Education, Values in the Family, Other Applications and An Annotated Bibliography on Value Clarification. Items 13, 15, 18, 19, 21, 22, 23, 30, 33, 34, 35, 36, 38, 47, 52, 53, 56, 58, 61, 63, 64, 68, 88, 95, 132, and 142 from this bibliography are included. In addition excerpts from 42, 43, and 44 are found, as well as articles by Kohlberg, Holt, Rogers, Rokeach, and others.

92. Mears, M. Who's Sid Simon and what's all this about values clarification? *Media and Methods*, 1973, *9*(7), 30–37.

   The author describes what value clarification is and why he feels it is a meaningful approach. He quotes frequently from *Values and Teaching* and includes descriptions and examples of several strategies, including Twenty Things I Love To Do, Value Grid, Value Voting, Rank Order, Public Interview, Time Journal, and Proud Whip.

93. McBride, A. Values are back in the picture. *America*, 1973, *128*(15), 359–361.

   Initially, the article explores the prominent position of values in education today. The work of Sidney B. Simon, who has popularized the value clarification movement is listed. The author notes, however, that value-clarification "games" do not answer such questions as "Is it true or false, good or bad?" He feels that judgment and decision are central to value education and must follow value clarification. The article concludes with a discussion of values in Catholic school and religious education.

94. Osman, J. D. A rationale for using value clarification in health education. *Journal of School Health*, 1973, *43*(10), 621–623.

The author summarizes the major aspects of value clarification—the need for it, the seven processes of valuing, the three levels of teaching, the strategies—and argues for the use of value clarification in health-education curricula. He concludes with a listing of advantages for the value-clarification approach.

95. Osman, J. D. Teaching nutrition with a focus on values. *Nutrition News*, 1973, *36*(2), 5.

Using the three-levels concept of teaching and the seven processes of valuing, Osman argues for the use of value clarification in nutrition education. He describes four value strategies for doing so, titled a "Dual Continuum" on the subjects of Nutrition and Weight, an adaptation of Twenty Things I Love To Do, called "Ten Foods I Love To Eat and Drink," Value Voting, and Rank Ordering.

96. Poetker, J. A strategy for value clarification. *Social Science Record*, Autumn 1973, *11*(1), 3–5.

A sequential, problem-solving approach is offered as a strategy for the classroom teacher who wants to help students increase their skills of inquiry, conceptual learning, and value clarification.

97. Roberts, D. F., & Roberts, G. Techniques for confronting sex-role stereotyping. *School Psychology Digest*, Summer 1973, 47–54.

After emphasizing the need to examine traditional sex-role stereotypes, the authors present Value Voting, Continua, and the Value Whip (or Circle Topics) as ways of helping students meet this objective. Many examples of these strategies are provided.

98. Sadker, D., Sadker, M., & Simon, S. Clarifying sexist values. *Social Education*, 1973, *37*(8), 756–760.

A variety of value-clarification strategies are presented as a crucial element in a teacher-preparation program designed to help teachers confront sexist values. Many of the strategies may be used by teachers to help elementary and secondary students clarify sexist values.

99. Simon, S. Star trek. In D. Briggs (Ed.), *Breaking Out*. New York: David McKay, 1973.

Five value-clarification strategies are presented that incorporate the value-clarification theory into the valuing process. It has a personal rather than professional focus. The strategies include Twenty Things I Love To Do, "I Learned" Statements, Baker's Dozen, Weekly Reaction Sheet, and Personal Coat of Arms.

100. Simon, S. B. Values and teaching. *Religious Education*, 1973, *68*(2), 183–194.

In this transcript of a live presentation, Simon discusses some of his own values and the consequences of these in his life. He then conducts a strategies demonstration of Voting, Ranking, "I Urge" Telegram, and "I Wonder" Statements with a panel of students.

101. Simon, S. B. Values clarification—a tool for counselors. *Personnel and Guidance Journal*, 1973, *51*(9), 614–618.

A brief introduction followed by several strategies including Either-Or Forced Choice, Spread of Opinion, Alternative Search, Twenty Things I Love To Do, "I Learned" Statements, and Opposite Quadrangles.

102. Simon, S. B. A values clarifier looks at poverty. *Issues Today*, 1973, *5*(14), 1–2.

The use of Sensitivity Modules and other strategies are included that focus on the subject of poverty.

103. Simon, S. B., & Goodman, J. Values clarification: Focus on work and leisure. *Today's Catholic Teacher*, 1973, *7*(1), 11–15.

Two strategies—"Favorites" and "Coat of Arms"—are presented as examples of how to help students explore the value rich areas of work and leisure. The Coat of Arms is described at some length, with several variations and follow-up steps.

104. Simon, S. B., & Goodman, J. Ways of teaching/learning. *Adult Leader*, 1973, *6*(1).

This reference includes a series of five articles. In the first, "Values Shock," the authors describe the nature of value shock, suggest an approach for dealing with it and offer an activity in affirmation. The second article, "I Love to . . . ," includes strategies to help people develop self-scientist inventorying skills. The third, "Values Clarification: Focus on Holidays" provides three activities (Holiday Autobiography, Past Christmas Inventory, and Christmas Gift Giving) to help explore the value-rich area of holidays. Three additional strategies (Are You Someone Who . . . ?, Percentage Stands, and Product Code) are described in the fourth article, "Values Clarification: Focus on Money." The final article, "Searching for Values," offers a conceptual summary of the open-accept-clarify valuing process.

105. Simon, S. B., & Hart, L. Values clarification. *Learning With Adults*, 1973, *1*(6), 15–18.

Listed are strategies to use in adult Bible classes and church leadership.

106. Simon, S. B., & Hart, L. Values clarification making your new year better. *Cross Talk*, 1973, *2*(4).

Five value-clarification strategies are presented to make New Year's resolutions for the next seventy years more effective. The strategies included are High Points Calendar, Twenty Things I Love To Do, "I Learned" Statements, New Year's Resolutions, and Self-Contract.

107. Simon, S. B., & Hartwell, M. Values clarification: A heritage of wisdom. *Curriculum Trends*, January 1973.

The amount of television watching that children do—they average 350,000 commercials by age seventeen—is offered as a graphic indicator of the need to help young people sort out all their input. Value clarification is used as one technique for dealing with this concern. Several methods of doing this are described, including the following: three-levels teaching, using *Macbeth* as an example; the Value Continuum, with the issue of seatbelts as the example; and Value Sheets, featuring an example titled "Ecology and Its Implications."

108. Simon, S. B., Hawley, R., & Britton, D. *Composition for personal growth: Values clarification through writing.* Amherst, Mass.: Education Research Associates, 1971, & New York: Hart Publishing, 1973.

A large number of value-clarification and personal-growth activities are suggested to encourage students to begin writing about themselves, their feelings, their thoughts and opinions, and their values. The activities are designed and structured to make writing a comfortable, enjoyable, and successful experience that will lead to more effective written communication. A rationale and a theoretical background for the teacher are provided.

109. Simon, S., & Massey, S. Values clarification: A strategy in the search for self. *Educational Leadership*, 1973, *30*(8), 738–739.

The Are You Someone Who . . . ? strategy is described and many variations and examples of how it might be used are given.

110. Smith, M. Some implications of value clarification for organization development. In J. W. Pfeiffer and J. E. Jones (Eds.), *The 1973 annual handbook for group facilitators*. La Jolla, Calif.: University Associates, 1973.

After summarizing the value-clarification theory, Smith presents two typical value-clarification strategies, both involving ranking, that help an individual clarify personal and professional priorities. He then shows how these kinds of strategies can be used in organizational settings to help groups negotiate expectations, establish goals and priorities, screen job candidates, and build teams.

111. Thal, H. M., & Holcombe, M. Value clarification. *American Vocational Journal*, 1973, *48*(9), 25–29.

The use of value clarification as an important component of any vocational education program is advocated. The more relaxed atmosphere of a vocational classroom provides a natural setting for the inclusion of value clarification along with the other elements of the regular vocational education program. The authors note that one positive result of such an approach is the spark of motivation provided to previously apathetic students. Twenty Things I Love To Do is presented as a sample strategy.

112. Watergate emphasizes need to teach ways of choosing values. *Pennsylvania School Journal*, September 1973, 20–22.

    The idea that recent socio-political events have stimulated a rebirth in value education is explored. Several examples of specific school efforts to incorporate the process of value clarification with students, teachers, and parents are noted. There is a brief description of how value clarification can be adapted for use in teaching subject matter.

113. Weber, Sister H. *Value prompters*. Denver, Colo.: Colorado Council of Churches, 1973.

    A series of cards with reaction statements, open-ended statements, situational dilemmas, and so on. Students choose a card, and either alone, in small groups, or in front of the entire group, respond according to their values. Religious, secular, and other topics are included. These discussion-starter cards are packaged in four separate sets for Catholic, Protestant, Jewish, and general interest groups.

114. Wilson, V., & Wattenmaker, B. *Can we humanize foreign language education?* Upper Jay, N.Y.: National Humanistic Education Center, 1973.

    A rationale for using value clarification and other humanistic approaches in teaching foreign languages is presented. In the introduction the authors describe their "Real Communication" approach, which employs the value-clarification theory.

115. Wilson, V., & Wattenmaker, B. *Real communication in foreign language*. Upper Jay, N.Y.: National Humanistic Education Center, 1973.

    Ways to use value clarification and other humanistic education approaches in teaching foreign languages to first- and second-year language classes are illustrated.

116. Wilson, V. & Wattenmaker, B. *Real communications in Spanish*. Upper Jay, N.Y.: National Humanistic Education Center, 1973.

    Ways to use value clarification and other humanistic education approaches to teach first- and second-year Spanish classes are described.

117. Wolfe, D., & Howe, L. Personalizing foreign language instruction. *Foreign Language Annals*, 1973, 7(1), 81–90.

    The decline in the popularity of foreign language study is inversely correlated with the increased need for humanizing education. Several value-clarification strategies are presented with ways of incorporating them into foreign language instruction. Examples include the following: Value Grid, Twenty Things I Love To Do, Value Voting, Rank Order, Unfinished Sentences, Public Interview, "I Urge" Telegrams, Letters to the Editor, The Fall-Out Shelter Problem, The Personal Life Map, and the Here-and-Now Wheel.

1974

118. Barman, C. Value clarification and biology. *The American Biology Teacher*, 1974, *36*(4), 241–242.

    The need for classroom science teachers to include controversial and value-laden issues in their teaching is presented. The issue of mercy killing is discussed. Other examples from science eduation are mentioned to assist educators in moving their teaching emphasis from the fact and concept levels to the value-clarification or "you" level.

119. Berger, B., Hopp, J. W., & Raettig, V. Values clarification and the cardiac patient. *Health Education Monographs*, Summer 1974, *3*(2), 191–199.

    This exploratory study tested the feasibility and potential of value-clarification methods in patient education with twenty chronic heart patients participating in the cardiac classes of a university medical center. The investigators concluded that value clarification appears to be an effective educational approach for many cardiac patients.

120. Betof, E., & Kirschenbaum, H. A valuing approach. *School Health Review*, 1974, *5*(1), 13–14.

    An abridgement of the authors' 1973 article. See entry #75 of this bibliography.

121. Bolton, R. *Values clarification for educators*. Cazenovia, N.Y.: Ridge Consultants, 1974.

    The book provides people with a needed background of valuing processes for workshop planning. It also presents guidelines for workshops, outlines the author's conception of the valuing process, describes valuing as a triple encounter (with self, with others, and with society), quotes a YMCA report relating valuing to education, and includes a bibliography.

122. Casteel, J. D., Stahl, R. J., Adkinson, M., & Gadsden, T. W., Jr. *Value clarification in social studies: Six formats of the values sheet*, Gainesville, Fla.: Florida Educational Research and Development Council, University of Florida, 1974.

    A publication using the Value Sheet format for combining the content and value levels of social studies teaching.

123. Curwin, R., Curwin, G., et al. *Developing individual values in the classroom*. Palo Alto, Calif.: Learning Handbooks, 1974.

    The book is devoted to the following issues: (a) explaining the meaning of value clarification, (b) presenting new value-clarification strategies that include examples of discussion questions to follow up the strategies, (c) showing how to integrate values in curriculum areas with examples provided for language arts, social studies, science, and math, (d) illustrating how to create new value-clarification activities, (e) detailing how to use self-evaluation, and (f) giving an annotated bibliography of fifty-four titles on value clarification and humanistic education.

124. Curwin, R., & Fuhrmann, B. *Discovering your teaching self.* Englewood Cliffs, N.J.: Prentice-Hall, 1974.

A book of value-clarification and other strategies to help teachers and educators think through their values and value priorities as professionals and enhance their professional self-concepts.

125. Dreischmeiers, W. B. Teaching for a change in attitude: Values clarification. *Agricultural Education Magazine*, December 1974, 129–130.

The ideas of Raths, Harmin, and Simon are presented to teachers of agriculture. It challenges them to use value clarification with their students.

126. Evans, C. Facing up to values. *Teacher*, 1974, *92*(4), 16–18 ; 72–73.

After listing the many reasons why teachers are fearful of getting involved with values discussions, the author describes how he conducts such discussions. Evans provides many specific guidelines that are helpful in value-clarification classrooms or groups.

127. Forcinelli, J., & Engeman, T. Value education in the public school. *Thrust*, October 1974, *4*(1), 13–16.

The authors briefly discuss the issue of whether value education should be taught in schools. Two reasons are offered in support of a school value-education program. Four value-oriented programs are reviewed: value clarification (Simon and Raths), cognitive-developmental (Lawrence Kohlberg), lifeline (Peter McPhail), and character education (American Institute of Character Education, San Antonio, Texas). Finally, the authors evaluate each program according to a set of personal criteria.

128. Genge, B. A. & Santosuosso, J. Values clarification for ecology. *Science Teacher*, 1974, *41*(2), 37–39.

A detailed look at how to use the Rank Ordering strategy with study topics related to pollution. Many variations and follow-up activities are suggested.

129. Green, J. One thing I wish Mr. Green did more of is . . . *Humanistic Educators Network*, 1974, *1*(2).

The trials and tribulations of a beginning teacher who uses value clarification.

130. Harmin, M. *Value cassettes: Making sense of our lives series.* Niles, Ill.: Argus Communications, 1974.

Six story-song activities on three cassette tapes described by the publisher as, "Powerful learning experiences, effective even with the least motivated of groups." The first five activities are built around value-clarifying issues including the problem of hunger, the gift of idealism, Dear Merrill, personal relationships, and a parent-child crisis. The sixth provides training in the no-lose conflict resolution model.

131. Harmin, M. *Process posters: Making sense of our lives series.* Niles, Ill.: Argus Communications, 1974.

Fifteen large, colorful posters outline processes that build humanistic classrooms. Example topics include "I Learned" Statements, active-listening pairs, support-group tasks, thinking assignments, the conflict resolution model, elements for learning contracts, writing critique suggestions, effective communication hints, and seven others.

132. Harmin, M., & Gregory, T. *Teaching is.* Chicago: Science Research Associates, 1974.

A combination of interesting readings about education and thirty-five value-clarification experiences to help teachers clarify their own professional values and their view of themselves as educators.

133. Hopp, J. Value clarification for sixth graders. *School Health Review*, 1974, *5*(1), 34–35.

More an editorial than an article, it suggests the time is ripe for applying value clarification to the area of health education. The title is misleading, as sixth graders are not the focus of the article.

134. Huggins, K. B. Alternatives in values clarification. *The National Elementary Principal*, 1974, *54*(2), 76–79.

A major portion of this article discusses how the value-clarification process is enhanced when students are permitted to choose freely, thoughtfully, and from alternatives. Coat of Arms, Role Playing, and Public Interviews are mentioned as illustrations. The author discusses how value clarification relates to student cognitive-developmental learning and to students' psychological need for direction..

135. Jones, C. Can schools teach ethics? *The Christian Science Monitor*, December 23, 1974, 1–2.

A look at how value clarification and moral development is being taught in the schools with some commentary on both approaches.

136. Kingman, B. *The development of value clarification skills: Initial efforts in an eighth grade social studies class.* Stony Brook, N.Y.: State University of New York, American Historical Association Education Project, 1974.

A description is made of the methods and problems found in implementing value clarification. Two strategies, the Clarifying Response and Value Sheets, are given particular focus and related to an eighth-grade social studies class. Systematic measures of classroom effects are closely considered and ways for accomplishing meaningful record-keeping are suggested and developed.

137. Kirschenbaum, H. *Recent research in values clarification*. Upper Jay, N.Y.: National Humanistic Education Center, 1974. Reprinted in Meyer, J., Burnham, B., & Cholvat, J. (Eds.), *Values education: Theory, practice, problems, prospects*. Waterloo, Ontario: Wilfred Laurier University Press, 1975.

The author discusses the research trends in value clarification and describes eleven newer studies titled (a) Outcomes of Values Clarification on Students and Target Populations, (b) Outcomes of Teacher Training in Values Clarification, and (c) Methodological Developments.

138. Kirschenbaum, H., & Simon, S. Values and the futures movement in education. In A. Toffler (Ed.), *Learning for tomorrow: The role of the future in education*. New York: Vintage Books, 1974.

A summary of value confusion, various ways of working with values, and the valuing process are discussed. Additionally, there is a description of schools that have (a) incorporated value clarification and humanistic approaches into existing courses, (b) created new courses with a humanistic or value focus, and (c) reorganized the school to allow for humanistic emphases.

139. Knapp, C., & DuShane, J. Clarifying values for a better environment. *Counseling and Values*, Summer 1974, *18*(4), 266–271.

A framework for examining value clarification within the context of ecological decisions is provided. Environmental examples are used to illustrate six specific strategies, which include Value Grid, Value Voting, Physical Continuum, Rank Ordering, Twenty Things I Love To Do, and Value Sheet. The article lists ten underlying assumptions of value clarification as practiced by many of its proponents. An environmental value-clarification bibliography is included.

140. Morrison, E., & Price, M. U. *Values in sexuality: A new approach to sex education*. New York: Hart, 1974.

Forty strategies for education in human sexuality are listed, of which most are of the value clarification type. Activities are grouped under the headings of Group-Building, Physiology, Psychosexual Development, Sex Roles, Values Clarification, Dimensions in Relationships, Nonmarital Sex, Marriage and Parenthood, Discussion Starters, and Summarizing Activities.

141. Nash, R. & Shiman, D. The English teacher as questioner. *English Journal*, December 1974, *63*(9), 38–44.

The authors describe a three-levels approach to teaching poetry and asking questions. They call their levels factual, conceptual, and contextual. The latter is similar to the value level.

142. Osman, J. D. The use of selected value clarifying strategies in health education. *Journal of School Health*, 1974, *44*(1), 21–25.

The author reviews his doctoral research in which he measured the effects of value clarification on several groups of education students. He presents many examples of Value Sheets and Thought Cards to illustrate two of the twenty valuing strategies the students experienced. He mentions what measures and tests he used and their results.

143. Osman, J., & Kenny, B. Value growth through drug education. *School Health Review*, 1974, *5*(1), 25–30.

The authors review the seven processes of valuing and present several strategies including Value Sheets titled "Drugs and Dogs," "Do You Mind If I Smoke?" "Alcoholism," and "Doctors, Drugs and You," Twelve Rank Orders on drugs and health, and an inventory called "The Drugs I Use."

144. Paulson, Wayne. *Deciding for myself: A values clarification series*. Minneapolis, Minn.: Winston Press, 1974.

For use with older elementary pupils, high-school-aged students, and adults, this series consists of thirty eight-page booklets. Each one contains a series of value-clarification activities. There are ten booklets in each of three sets. Set A, "Clarifying My Values" has booklets with activities on such valuing processes as prizing, alternatives, and speaking out. Set B helps the user examine everyday choices including relationships, possessions, money, and leisure. Set C, "Where Do I Stand?" focuses on such social issues as environment, poverty, and drugs. The *Leader's Guide*, which can be used with or without the series, serves as a useful tool for implementing value-clarification activities in classes or groups.

145. Santosuosso, J. Should schools deal in values clarification? *The Watman Educational Services Bulletin*, 1974, *3*(10), 2.

A description of how to prevent value clarification from becoming repetitive and gimick-like with students is presented.

146. Schlaadt, R. Implementing the values clarification process. *School Health Review*, 1974, *5*(1), 10–12.

After briefly introducing the seven valuing processes and some guidelines for using value clarification in the classroom, Schlaadt presents several strategies with health-education content including Value Grid, Value Continuum, Value Sheet, Personal Coat of Arms, and a strategy titled "Tied Down."

147. Simon, S. B. *Meeting yourself halfway*. Niles, Ill.: Argus Communications, 1974.

Thirty-one value-clarification strategies are adapted for general use. The introduction to the book and instructions for each activity are designed to allow the reader to use the strategies alone or with a group of friends.

148. Simon, S. Talking to parents about values clarification. *The Watman Education Services Bulletin*, 1974, *3*(10), 1–2.

Ideas are presented about how to respond to parents who object to the school becoming involved with value education.

149. Simon, S. B. *Values in teaching*. Dayton, Ohio: Creative Sights and Sounds, 1974.

Two cassette tapes of Simon's 1971 presentation to the Ohio Catholic Education Association in which he describes some of the innovations at the School of Education at the University of Massachusetts, discusses some drawbacks of the traditional grading system, and conducts a panel with high school students demonstrating the Voting, Ranking, Continuum, "I Urge" Telegram, "I Wonder" Statements, and Public Interview strategies. Simon weaves value-clarification theory into his demonstration.

150. Simon, S. B., & Bohn, M. B. What schools should be doing about values clarification. *The National Association of Secondary School Principals Bulletin*, 1974, *58*(379), 54–60.

A brief introduction is included with the following strategies: Name Tags, Twenty Things I Love To Do, "I Learned" Statements, Brown Bag, Weekly Reaction Questions, Proud Whip, Lifeline, Who Am I?, Obituary, and Two Perfect Days.

151. Simon, S. B., Sadker, M., & Sadker, D. Where do they stand? *Instructor*, 1974, *84*(1), 110; 112; 119.

Five strategies on the issue of sexism are noted, including Value Voting, Rank Orders, Value Continuum, Unfinished Sentences, and Diaries.

152. Stoller, P., Lock, J., Wilson, V., & Wattenmaker, B. *Real communication in French*. Upper Jay, N.Y.: National Humanistic Education Center, 1974.

This book discusses how to use value clarification and other humanistic education approaches in teaching first- and second-year French classes.

153. Superka, D. Approaches to values education. *Social Science Education Consortium Newsletter*, November 1974, *20*.

The author mentions some of the problems facing value education in general and describes eight different approaches to value education titled evocation, inculcation, awareness, moral reasoning, analysis, clarification, commitment, and union. For each approach, the purposes, methods, and an illustrative activity are provided.

154. Warren, C. L. Value strategies in mental health. *School Health Review*, 1974, *5*(1), 22–24.

Following a brief introduction, Warren describes four strategies including a Public Interview, Voting, IALAC, and Twenty Things I Love To Do. Three of the four strategies contain moralistic examples.

155. Wilkinson, C. Value learning replaces school religious classes. *The Calgary Herald*, September 14, 1974, p.38.

The author reports that the value-clarification movement, initiated in the United States, is spreading and growing throughout Canada. Interest and support for value education has been so strong that an amendment to the Consolidated Education Act was passed by the Canadian government to officially endorse the teaching of value education in schools. Wilkinson further notes that the work of Simon, Howe, and Kirschenbaum has directly assisted Canadian educators in providing an effective, challenging, and meaningful program of value clarification in their classrooms. Examples of classroom strategies are outlined and discussed.

1975

156. Barman, C. Integrating value clarification with high school biology. *The American Biology Teacher*, 1975, *37*(3), 150–153.

Several value sheets, questions, and continua are presented that integrate value clarification and high school biology. The author then details a research experiment to determine if an experimental group of high school students exposed to biology lessons that have been integrated with value-clarification strategies would achieve higher academically in their biology course than a comparison group of students who were not exposed to value-clarification strategies. Results showed that the academic achievement of the experimental group was greater even though there were no differences in attitude toward science and biology between the two groups.

157. Blaeuer, D. A. Student teaching and the valuing process. *New Directions in Teaching*, Winter 1975, *4*(4).

The author describes how he employed value clarification with student teachers of mathematics. He used value-clarification activities in both their pre-student teaching work and in their classroom supervision.

158. Casteel, J. D., & Stahl, R. J. *Value clarification in the classroom: A primer*. Pacific Palisades, Calif.: Goodyear Publishing, 1975.

An entire book on the Value Sheet strategy. It contains no references to previous value-clarification work or theory and many value sheets have few third-level questions. Still, ideas are offered for using Value Sheets, especially in the social studies area.

159. Colby, A. Book review. *Harvard Educational Review*, 1975, *45*(1), 134–143.

The author reviews *Values and Teaching* and *Values Clarification: A Handbook of Practical Strategies*. Colby compares the value-clarification theory to Kohlberg's theory of moral development. The article concludes that in some ways the moral development and value clarification approaches do conflict, but it is possible to use them in a complementary manner without being inconsistent.

160. Curwin, G. & Curwin, R. Building trust: A starting point for clarifying values. *Learning*, 1975, *3*(6), 30–33; 36.

This article, excerpted from the book *Developing Individual Values in the Classroom* (#123), describes how the value-clarification process helps students meet their need to find meaning and order in their social environment. The authors describe a three-stage process for building trust. The major portion of the article is devoted to describing nine new strategies as a beginning for clarifying values and building trust among students.

161. Desrosiers, M., & Santosuosso, J. *Personalizing the study of foreign cultures*. Upper Jay, N.Y.: National Humanistic Education Center, 1975.

Using India as their prototype, the authors show how value-clarification strategies can help the study of a foreign culture take on a personal meaning for students. This is one of the most complete examples of a three-levels curriculum unit in value-clarification literature. Examples of strategies used include Value Sheets, Inventories, and Interviewing.

162. Fiske, E. New techniques help pupils develop values. *New York Times*, April 30, 1975, p.33.

A description of how the value-clarification and moral-development approaches are being used in American education. Excerpts from interviews with Sidney Simon and Lawrence Kohlberg are woven into the article.

163. Goodman, J. & Walker, M. Values clarification: Helping people to feel more value–able. *Ohio's Health*, September, 1975, 11–15.

Describing value clarification as filling the need for (a) a wholistic approach, (b) self-literacy, and (c) combating devaluation, the authors proceed to describe three-level learning, revolving around the themes of self-worth and smoking.

164. Gray, R. D., III. They still go to the bathroom in platoons: An interview with Louis E. Raths. *Humanistic Educators Network*, 1975, *1*(7).

The "founder" of value clarification reminisces about his early work in formulating his values theory and method, and shares some views on how the approach developed subsequently.

165. Green, K. Values clarification theory in ESL and bilingual education. *Teaching English as a Second Language Quarterly*, 1975, *9*(2), 155–164.

Not available for annotation.

166. Greenberg, J. S. Behavior modification and values clarification and their research implications. *Journal of School Health*, 1975, *45*(2), 91–95.

Behavior modification and value clarification are discussed, the two methodologies are defined, conditions under which they are best conducted are described, contrasts and similarities between the two methods are drawn, and potential for research is mentioned.

167. Hardin, J. Values clarification, micro-counseling, education of the self and achievement motivation training: A critique. *Meforum*, University of Massachusetts School of Education, Spring 1975, 30–36.

A brief summary of these four approaches is presented and their pros and cons are delineated.

168. Hawley, R. *Value exploration through role playing*. New York: Hart, 1975.

A description is presented of various ways for using role playing to encourage value-clarification and subject-matter learning in the classroom. Ideas on "what to do when things go wrong" and how role playing relates to the development of moral judgment are included.

169. Hawley, R., & Hawley, I. *Human values in the classroom: A handbook for teachers*. New York: Hart, 1975.

The authors show how to use value-clarification and personal-growth activities sequenced according to the following seven teaching concerns: Orientation, Community Building, Achievement Motivation, Fostering Open Communication, Information Seeking and Sharing, Values Exploration and Clarification, and Planning for Change. Familiar activities are included but newer ones are cited. (This is a revised and expanded version of the 1973 edition—same title—published by Education Research Associates.)

170. Howe, L., & Howe, M. M. *Personalizing education: Values clarification and beyond*. New York: Hart, 1975.

A major publication showing how to integrate and sequence value-clarification activities in order to (a) build trust and good human relations in a group, (b) help students clarify their goals and purposes with respect to the group or class, (c) personalize the curriculum, and (d) handle ongoing classroom management, organization, record keeping, and so on. Over 100 strategies, worksheets, and sample units are listed including many new ones.

171. Johnson, P. Understanding and using values. *1975 YMCA yearbook and official roster*. New York: National Board of Young Men's Christian Association, 1975.

The author defines values and valuing, identifies the sources of values, and explores some of the problems people face in having values guide their behavior. She describes several approaches toward value education, including inculcation, analysis, clarification, and commitment. She also discusses problems that groups and individuals have in dealing with values and offers suggestions for overcoming them.

172. Kirschenbaum, H. *Clarifying values clarification: Some theoretical issues*. Upper Jay, N.Y.: National Humanistic Education Center, 1975.

A description of the author's expanded conception of the valuing process includes the five dimensions and sub-processes of thinking, feeling, choosing, communicating, and acting. A new formulation of the valuing process is presented.

173. Kirschenbaum, H. *Current research in values clarification*. Upper Jay, N.Y.: National Humanistic Education Center, 1975.

A revision and expansion of the author's 1974 research summary (#137), which contains eight new studies and further information on two previously reported studies.

174. Kirschenbaum, H., Harmin, M., Howe, L., & Simon, S. B. In defense of values clarification: A position paper. *Humanistic Educators Network*, 1975, *1*(7).

Four value-clarification leaders respond to criticism of value clarification. They carefully outline the value-clarification theory and discuss the charges that value clarification is value free, relativistic, superficial, and without a theoretical or research foundation. This is the most recent, concise, and penetrating summary of value-clarification theory in print to date.

175. Knapp, C. & Warren, L. Outdoor environmental values clarification. *Environmental Education Report*, February 1975, p.8.

An activity is described showing how teachers or group leaders can help students and others engage in outdoor environmental value clarification.

176. Kohlberg, L. The relationship of moral education to the broader field of values education. In J. Meyer, B. Burnham, & J. Cholvat (Eds.), *Values education: Theory, practice, problems and prospects*. Waterloo, Ontario: Wilfred Laurier University Press, 1975.

Kohlberg points out that moral education is one form of value education. He suggests that value clarification is a very valuable approach in the area of general values education. In comparing the two theories, however, he sees value clarification as "relativistic" and, therefore, inadequate.

177. Lockwood, A. A critical view of values clarification. *Teachers College Record*, 1975, 77(1), 35–50.

The author criticizes three aspects of value clarification, including (a) its definition of a value, and the role of action, (b) the value clarification concept of effective treatment for value confusion, and (c) value clarification's amoral or relativistic point of view.

178. Morel, S. *Human dynamics in foreign language series: Human dynamics in Italian: Teacher's manual and student workbook.* Saratoga Springs, N.Y.: National Humanistic Education Center, 1975.

This series is designed for advanced foreign language classes. The workbooks have forty value-clarification and personal-growth activities for students to complete in the foreign language. The teacher's manuals include an introduction to the Human Dynamics approach, copies of all the student activity worksheets, and instructions for facilitating each strategy. (German, French and Spanish editions are also available.)

179. Rokeach, M. Toward a philosophy of value education. In J. Meyer, B. Burnham, & J. Cholvat (Eds.), *Values education: Theory, practice, problems, prospects.* Waterloo, Ontario: Wilfred Laurier University Press, 1975.

A discussion of value clarification is presented in which the author criticizes several aspects of the value-clarification theory but not its method. He questions the "all or nothing" criteria for a value and the so-called "value neutrality" of value clarification. In spite of these criticisms, he credits value clarification with establishing the importance of dealing with values in the curriculum. "Such a broadening of educational objectives," he says, "now has a universal face validity, largely because of the pioneering work of proponents of values clarification."

180. Simon, S. B., & Clark, J. *Beginning values clarification: Strategies for the classroom.* (Note: First printing was titled *More values clarification.*) San Diego, Calif.: Pennant Press, 1975.

Thirty-three clarification strategies (some new, some variations on earlier ones) are presented.

181. Simon, S. B., & deSherbinin, P. Values clarification: It can start gently and grow deep. *Phi Delta Kappan*, 1975, 56(10), 679–683.

The authors point out the need for value clarification, list some of its outcomes, and present different examples of how it has been used in educational and other settings.

182. Simon, S. B., & O'Rourke, R. Getting to know you. *Educational Leadership*, 1975, *32*(8), 524–526.

The authors stress that the basis for effective learning lies in the willingness and ability of classroom teachers to make themselves known to the students and for the students to make themselves known to their teachers. As a result, mutual needs can be brought to an awareness level and, hopefully, reciprocally met. The article illustrates four value-clarification strategies to assist teachers and students in revealing themselves to one another. The strategies include What I Believe, Life Inventory, Contract with Myself, and My Personal Story.

183. Smith, M. (Ed.). *Retreat resources: Volume I: Retreats for clergy and religions.* New York: Paulist Press, 1975.

The author weaves ten value-clarification strategies into this book and adapts them for use on religious retreats. Coat of Arms, Twenty Things I Love To Do, and "I Urge" Telegrams are illustrated.

184. Stewart, J. S. Clarifying values clarification. *Phi Delta Kappan*, 1975, *56*(10), 684–688.

The author strongly criticizes value clarification in general and the Simon-deSherbinin article (#180) in particular. Stewart sees value clarification as superficial, theoretically inconsistent, potentially harmful, and lacking a solid research base.

185. Superka, D., Johnson, P. L., & Ahrens, C. *Values education: Approaches and materials.* Boulder, Colo.: ERIC Clearinghouse for Social Studies/Social Science Education and the Social Science Education Consortium, 1975.

The authors provide a typology of various value-education approaches (which includes value clarification), discuss how value-education materials are analyzed, examine various materials that represent the different approaches, and provide a bibliography on values and value-education materials.